"I hear participants of May McCarthy's workshops, weeks after the workshop, exclaim about their increase of success and joy on an ongoing basis as a result of the simple success tools outlined in her book. Not only are business owners talking about increased success, but everyone is talking about the increased sweetness of their personal relationship to a higher power. The tools are imminently practical and so easy and fun to apply."

— ILEANA VASSILIOU
President of Creating
Effective Organizations, Inc.

"May McCarthy is a prosperity genius. She has developed a clear prosperity plan that is easy to implement. She provides all readers with a complete recipe for financial success. Now that we have the recipe, it is up to each of us to engage in the discipline of delight to implement it."

— DR. TOM SANNAR
Senior Minister & Spiritual Director
One Heart-One Mind Center for Spiritual Living, San Diego, CA

"May McCarthy presents solid spiritual principles wrapped in a most delightful and engaging package. She is articulate, spiritually grounded, joy-filled and engaging. It just doesn't get any better than that!"

— REV. DR. MICHELE WHITTINGTON
Senior Spiritual Director
Creative Living Fellowship, Phoenix, AZ

"I would recommend any individual that is interested in meeting and exceeding more of their goals to read May's book."

— CYNTHIA CLAY
President & CEO
NetSpeed Learning Solutions
Author of: *Great Webinars: How to Create, Interactive Learning that is Captivating, Informative,* and *Fun and Peer Power: Transforming Workplace Relationships*

"May McCarthy's daily success practice has forever changed how I move and breathe in every moment within my business. My new daily practice shifted my relationship with Spirit into one that is very personal, safe and familiar. Since starting this process my business has grown dramatically. I am forever grateful for your introduction to the CSO and simple tools outlined in your book. It has changed my life!"

— MAKENA PHILLIPS
Founder
Shepard Moon Concoctions

THE GRATITUDE FORMULA

The Gratitude FORMULA

MAY McCARTHY

Hierophantpublishing

Cover design by Emma Smith
Cover photo by Michael Kleven Photography
Interior Design by Steve Amarillo / Urban Design LLC

Hierophant Publishing
8301 Broadway, Suite 219
San Antonio, TX 78209
210-305-5027
www.hierophantpublishing.com

If you are unable to order this book from your local bookseller, you may order directly from the publisher.

Library of Congress Control Number: 2017961462

ISBN: 978-1-938289-74-3
10 9 8 7 6 5 4 3 2 1
Printed on acid-free paper in United States

Gratitude can transform common days into thanksgivings, turn routine jobs into joy and change ordinary opportunities into blessings.

— WILLIAM ARTHUR WARD

Be thankful for what you have; you'll end up having more. If you concentrate on what you don't have, you will never, ever have enough.

— OPRAH WINFREY

CONTENTS

DEDICATION

This book is dedicated to my loving husband Don Smith. I am so grateful for the countless hours of discussion that you've had with me, the numerous drafts that you've read with constructive feedback, and the dozens of speaking and teaching events that you've traveled to with me to share the material in this book. You are truly a gift as my best friend and husband. Thank you so very much. I love you.

PREFACE

*Let us be grateful to the people who make
us happy; they are the charming gardeners who
make our souls blossom.*

— MARCEL PROUST

Grateful people are happier and healthier, and tend to be more successful in relationships! Think about the people that you like to spend time with. Don't they appear to be grateful for what they have—a good home, a great job, a beautiful family, a healthy life? Other people you know may tend to complain about everything they don't have. What type of person are you? When you see the water in the glass, do you view it as half empty or half full?

Gratitude is a choice. As you choose to develop a habit of being grateful, tremendous benefits will return to you. Canadian actor Will

Arnet said, "I am happy because I'm grateful. I choose to be grateful. That gratitude allows me to be happy." In choosing to be grateful, we become happier.

There is a significant amount of information available about the benefits of gratitude. In November, 2007, Dr. Blaire Justice and Dr. Rita Justice reported for the University of Texas Health Science Center Magazine, *Health Leader*, that "a growing body of research shows that gratitude is truly amazing in its physical and psycho-social benefits." When you review the dozens of articles that have been written on the topic, you'll find that numerous studies have shown that developing a gratitude habit is beneficial in a number of different ways. We deepen and expand relationships. Our physical and psychological health improves. We sleep better and are more at peace. We become more productive and creative. Our self-esteem improves as we reduce the number of social comparisons that we make. It's clear to me that being grateful can help us physically, socially, and mentally.

In addition to the wonderful health benefits that we receive from being grateful, I believe that gratitude is also a tool for success. It helps us to maintain the optimal state to notice more opportunities to achieve our goals. Being grateful also stimulates our subconscious and intuition to provide us with more information that is in alignment with our desired outcomes. We tend to notice helpful information more easily when we incorporate gratitude as a habit into our lives. As you implement gratitude as part of a daily success system, you will be able to achieve more of your goals and feel a greater sense of happiness in the process. That's something to feel grateful about!

In this book, I will share with you that success is not a secret known by only a few, it's a system that everyone can use. Part of that system is developing a gratitude habit. I will explain and help you practice the simple steps of the daily success system and introduce you to a new spiritual partner as the source of your intuition—your ultimate advisor—to direct you to achieve your goals. As you practice gratitude and your daily system for success, you'll find that there will be more for you to be grateful about during each day. Motivational speaker and author Brian Tracy summed it up perfectly when he said: "Develop an attitude of gratitude, and give thanks for everything that happens to you, knowing that every step forward is a step toward achieving something bigger and better than your current situation." The physical, mental, and social benefits of gratitude will be multiplied in your life while you achieve the desires of your heart. This often occurs in seemingly miraculous or unusual ways. Developing a gratitude habit may be the greatest improvement that you make in order to lead you to a wonderful life.

In addition to the daily success system, I will share the importance of using the right words, thoughts, and emotions to describe your completed goals. Words have power, and you will learn how to direct that power to illuminate more possibilities to joyfully realize your good life. I will show you how your beliefs have helped or hindered you in the past as well as the simple techniques that you can implement to create new beliefs that are in line with your goals. You'll learn to eliminate fears and doubts, and you'll experience proof that your new beliefs can attract what you want sooner. The tools in this book will help you to uncover your personal purpose and let it shine in every area of your life. This becomes the fuel and passion that keeps you motivated to achieve all that you desire, require, and more.

Life becomes a game of fun, health, happiness, and abundance as you move through life with gratitude. The American poet, Maya Angelou, said "This a wonderful day. I've never seen this one before." Each day, she expected wonderful things to occur and her ideas for success to be achieved. She realized the life she described and more. You can too! My hope is that you choose to develop a gratitude habit. As you do, you will see that there is more in life to be grateful for, and you will achieve more that you desire.

I'm grateful that you've chosen to read this book and am delighted that you're making a commitment to live the life that you design.

INTRODUCTION

There are only two ways to live your life. One is as though nothing is a miracle. The other is as though everything is a miracle.

— ALBERT EINSTEIN

Miracles abound! Many of us have been exposed to a variety of stories about apparent miracles. We hear about incredible cures for terminally diagnosed illnesses, homes left standing without damage after fierce storms, or we witness peaceful resolutions to conflicts that harmed families, friends, communities, and nations for years.

A miracle is defined as: "an extraordinary event that manifests with divine intervention in human affairs," or "an extremely outstanding or unusual event." Have you ever experienced an extremely outstanding or unusual event?

In December 1983, physician Rex Gardner published a study in the *British American Journal* (volume 287) that reviewed medical cases in which healing events took place that couldn't be explained scientifically. One case identified a student physician who was suddenly diagnosed with what is called Waterhouse-Friderichsen syndrome. This is a bacterial blood infection that leads to massive internal bleeding and is considered fatal. The hospital treating the patient had a zero percent success rate in curing this condition. Upon being admitted to the hospital, the patient's chest X-rays showed extensive pneumonia in her left side and a completely collapsed middle lobe in her lung. She also had developed intraocular bleeding, which left her completely blind in one eye. Shortly after learning this, four different spiritual groups actively sent healing intentions to the patient. Within a day, there was a drastic improvement in her condition. Forty-eight hours after the healing intentions began, the X-ray showed a perfectly clear chest, and she had regained full vision. According to modern day physicians, this was impossible.

Stories like these can encourage us to expect that miracles or extraordinary events can and should happen in all of our lives. As we make these kinds of stories familiar and welcome, we build up confidence that miracles are possible. As we remain hopeful, grateful, intentional, and focused on the successful outcomes that we desire—like the four spiritual groups did in the health related story above—we begin to look for evidence of extremely outstanding or unusual events all around us.

When I was a growing up as the youngest of ten children in Hawaii, I witnessed a number of extraordinary events that I'll call miracles. My sisters and brothers got into horrible car accidents and were unhurt when circumstances indicated that they shouldn't have even survived. I fractured my back while body surfing, and the doctor said that it was a miracle that I wasn't paralyzed for life. Friends' homes were left standing when terrible storms severely damaged all of the homes around them. Even our family priest was cured of cancer, after doctors had told him the month before that he wouldn't survive more than six months.

Everyone can agree that extraordinarily unusual or miraculous events happen. However, many of us have been conditioned to believe that there is an element of chance in their occurrence. Wouldn't it be wonderful if we could use a provable and repeatable system to enable these "extremely outstanding events" to happen more often? It's my belief that we can do simple things to notice more evidence of outstanding events happening. Using a daily system for success that incorporates the power of gratitude along with the use of spiritual and practical tools is the key.

In this book you will learn the importance of gratitude as a valuable part of a daily system for success so that you can experience more of the good things you desire. Whether you want greater financial freedom, improved health, satisfying work, harmonious relationships, or regular recreation and the means to enjoy it, you can use the daily system for success to enable you to receive all of these things and more. As you practice this success system on a daily basis, you will soon be able to see how miracles will become typical occurrences.

Over the past couple of years, I've had the pleasure and privilege to travel around the world sharing the success principles outlined in my previous book, *The Path to Wealth: Seven Spiritual Steps for*

Financial Abundance. I'm delighted that thousands of people are now experiencing greater abundance as they manifest more of their goals. They now understand that success and prosperity are available to everyone.

I'm frequently asked whether the daily practice described in *The Path to Wealth* can be used for manifesting non-financial goals as well. My answer is a resounding, "Yes!" In this book, I will describe the use of a daily practice to help you achieve both financial and non-financial goals, to build up your confidence, and to change limiting beliefs and behaviors that have prevented you from achieving what you want in every area of your life.

First, I think that it's important for you to understand my personal definition of wealth: "to be whole and complete, lacking nothing, in all areas of your life." This includes your health, relationships, personal development, recreational activities, finances, and your spiritual connection to the source and creative power of the universe.

This all-knowing power of the universe is available at all times to guide you to achieving your goals. In this book, you will learn more about the importance of partnering with this power so that you can receive helpful information that will easily and joyfully guide you to the life that you want. I find that it's helpful in the partnership to name the characteristic of this power which will direct you towards your completed goals through intuition, feelings, signs, and messages from other people. It is my pleasure to introduce you to my Chief Spiritual Officer.

THE CHIEF SPIRITUAL OFFICER

've affectionately named my spiritual partner the Chief Spiritual Officer, or CSO, and recognize that it is the ultimate advisor in my life. As a CEO of several companies, I've surrounded myself with people whose advice I value, such as my chief financial officer, my chief operations officer, and my chief information officer. All of these people are subject-matter experts who advise me about their areas of expertise for the benefit of our company, our coworkers, customers, suppliers, and vendors. I decided that the all-knowing power of the universe knew more than I did about everything, and could provide me with advice beyond my rational understanding. So, as I started my sixth company (which operated in the healthcare industry), I committed to partnering with this advisor and giving it a title: the Chief Spiritual Officer, or CSO for short. I placed the CSO at the top of my organizational chart so that I, as the CEO, reported to it.

Many of my employees asked who the CSO was, and whether it was a man or a woman. They wanted to know if they would get to meet him or her. I explained that they could consider the CSO a symbol and principle for us as a miracle-making company—a company that was going to experience outstanding and unusual events often. I shared my belief in using a daily system for success, and I asked them to stay focused on the outcomes that they wanted to achieve at all times. If they had a difficult problem, I asked them to focus on the successful outcome of having the problem resolved. If they had a challenge that they weren't expecting, I asked them to imagine how happy their life would be when the challenge was overcome. I explained that if they were grateful for the successful outcome they desired in advance, they would see more evidence and opportunities to take steps to achieve their goals.

It was no surprise to me that I received several texts, emails, and phone calls from my employees describing how intuitive and creative things happened to help them throughout each day. They were able to prove repeatedly that the CSO principle was guiding us to be a miracle-making company—a company that had "extremely outstanding and unusual events" happen on a regular basis.

You may call your valued advisor whatever name you choose. Many who attend my workshops choose names like God, Divine Intelligence, Power, Spirit, or other names that represent an ultimate advisor for them. The important point is that this all-knowing power of the universe is available as your partner and advisor to help you realize more of what you desire in life, while doing less of the work. There are simple things that you can do each day to enable your CSO to help you more often in more obvious ways. Success is not a secret, it's a system.

As you use gratitude and the daily success system in your partnership with your CSO, you will begin to receive directions through intuition, signs, messages from others, and strong ideas to take steps along a path to manifest your goals. Intuitive messages can show up as strong thoughts about someone to contact or someplace to go. You might have feelings in your gut, heart, or other parts of your body that give you direction to take action. You may receive a message from someone else that has meaning for you or see a sign that points the way. I'll provide more information and examples throughout this book that will help you notice and recognize these kinds of intuitive messages and how to utilize them for your benefit.

In your new partnership, you and your CSO will have separate roles and responsibilities to follow. Your job is to describe what you desire with gratitude as though you've already achieved it. The job of your CSO is to create the path for you to get there and to give you one step at a time towards your goal. You either take the action step or ask for another sign or lead. This is the hard part for some, since often we won't know the outcome of taking a step and may not be able to determine what goal is being addressed. This is where you need to show courage, as Steve Jobs advised when he said, "Have the courage to follow your heart and intuition. They somehow already know what you truly want to become. Everything else is secondary."

To illustrate how this works, let me share with you a story. In 1994, one of my goals was "to have a healthy, whole, and complete body that was physically fit, energetic, and filled with vitality." I was in the habit of using the daily system for success outlined in this book and was grateful in advance for achieving my goal.

One day in the middle of a business meeting, I had a flash or picture of my sister's face in my mind's eye. That's one of the ways that the CSO gives me intuitive messages, and I knew that I was being directed to take a step and contact my sister. I didn't know why or for what goal I was being guided to contact her, I just knew that I had to take a step or ask for another lead or clarification from my ultimate advisor, my CSO partner.

Since I was close to my sister's office, I decided to stop by. She was happy to see me; she had a computer problem that I could help her fix. As I was sitting at her desk, she asked me about a tiny spot on the outside of my right leg. I told her that it was a freckle. I have lots of freckles after being raised in Hawaii. She said that she didn't feel that it was a freckle and asked that I see her dermatologist to have it looked at.

Just as I was about to dismiss her fear and tell her that it was nothing to worry about, my gut hurt. That's another way that my CSO gives me intuitive leads and directions. So, I did as my sister advised and made the appointment.

During the examination, the doctor told me that the spot was nothing to worry about. He said that it was too small and that I could go home. Upon hearing this, I noticed a strong feeling in my gut which was trying to get my attention. I was also reminded of a strong belief that I developed when I was a child. My father was a surgeon who let his ten children know repeatedly that doctors knew more than we did and that we should always trust their advice. As I was about to heed the doctor's advice to get dressed and leave, my gut continued to hurt, so I faced my old belief about doctors always being right and asked the doctor to cut out the spot and have it analyzed.

A week later, I returned to the doctor's office to learn that I had a malignant melanoma, Clark's level III. Since the cancer was caught early, I was able to undergo simple surgery without radiation or ongoing treatment. The CSO guided me through thoughts, gut feelings, and messages through my sister to reach my goal for perfect health.

As you use the daily system for success with gratitude and learn to recognize and follow leads from your spiritual partner, you'll find that you can achieve more of what you want in life on a regular basis with less of the work. You'll prove that the daily system for success works as you experience unusual and extraordinary events more often. Miracles will become typical occurrences for which you can always be grateful.

I'm delighted that you've chosen to read this book so that you can enjoy the life that you desire filled with happiness, health, satisfaction, prosperity, great relationships, and more. To paraphrase one of my favorite nineteenth-century authors and teachers, Emma Curtis Hopkins, there is good for you and you ought to have it. I would add that you should have your good now.

Thank you for joining me on this journey to experience more good in your life.

SUCCESS IS A SYSTEM, NOT A SECRET

*That some achieve great success, is proof to
all that others can achieve it as well.*

— ABRAHAM LINCOLN

When you make the commitment to learn something new, don't you put in concerted mental and physical effort on a repeated basis to become proficient in the new task? You apply knowledge that's necessary to achieve the results that you desire. All of us have been using this kind of a system for success our entire lives.

For example, think about when you first learned to ride a bicycle.

Didn't you spend hours learning how to balance and move on the bike without falling? I can recall vividly the times that I crashed and fell off my bike while learning to ride on two wheels. I spent hours practicing what I was taught over and over. I watched family and friends ride their bikes without falling. I dreamed about sailing down the street, feeling the wind through my hair as I expertly rode my bike. Every day I thought about and practiced riding. When I made progress, I expressed tremendous gratitude. Once I believed strongly that it was possible to ride my bike without falling, things shifted and I began to see more evidence of my improvement.

Can you remember learning to type? At first, the keyboard was scary: it wasn't even in alphabetical order! Now after years of practice, maybe you're one of those people who is able to type without much thought. I know some teenagers who can type as fast as they can speak. Wow!

What about reading? Didn't you learn to sound out each word with great effort? Then you had to understand the meaning of the words, relate them to a sentence, a paragraph, and a story. Years later, having read countless numbers of words, you're most likely able to simply skim pages of words with the same successful understanding of their meaning.

I hope that you're beginning to recognize that success is a system. Champion auto racer, Bobby Unser shared, "*Success is where preparation and opportunity meet.*" As you continually prepare to be successful, you will notice more opportunities to achieve your goals. Both physical and mental repetition are key components of your preparation as part of the success system. In essence, repetition reaps rewards.

One of the best illustrations for this is the evening drive home from work. Have you ever driven home and had no awareness of large parts of the drive? This happens because you have become skilled at driving by repeating the behavior often. What was once a very conscious and deliberate effort has now become an ordinary and typical occurrence. Through repetition, you've mastered what you wanted to learn and developed a habit.

The same thing is true when using a new daily system for success to achieve more of your goals. Taking on the CSO as a new partner to help you and repetition of a daily practice with gratitude are necessary elements of your new system for success. As you incorporate and repeat the steps in your success system, you will find that it becomes easier for you to achieve more of your desired goals. Your goals can involve your health, happiness, relationships, work, finances, spiritual connection with your source, or any other achievement that you desire. It can take disciplined effort to get into a system of frequently manifesting goals, but, just like riding a bike or driving a car, it will get easier with practice. In some cases, these repetitive activities will become new habits over time.

Habits emerge through associative learning. University of Southern California professor Wendy Wood explained this in her session at the American Psychological Association's 122nd Annual Convention in 2014; "We find patterns of behavior that allow us to reach goals. We repeat what works, and when actions are repeated in a stable context, we form associations between cues and response." We can learn to repeat what works as a success system to reach our goals.

Types of Success Systems

There are a number of systems that people use to achieve success.

- In professional sports, athletes mentally and physically train every day to perform at the highest levels. The same is true for professional musicians.

- In religions and spiritual organizations, forms of prayer are used in a repetitive way along with gratitude, confidence, and faith. Prayer may include gratitude statements for achieving the outcomes desired in advance as well as the confidence that it can manifest. Repetitive chanting is often used to success-fully reach a deeper level of connection with a spiritual source that can provide directions and orchestrate opportunities to achieve desired outcomes.

- In business, leaders and managers set and revisit goals regu-larly and measure their efforts against them. Often, they will post their goals for performance, safety, or customer satisfac-tion where all employees can see them. This promotes an atti-tude of agreement.

In the daily system for success that I describe in this book, many of the most effective elements of the success systems above are com-bined into an efficient daily practice for the greatest results.

Look at the world's top athletes. They are known for practicing their routines, their workouts, and their skills a million times over in training, especially before big competitions. According to sports psychologist Michael Edgar, "Three (must have) keys to success in sports are good instruction, practice, and repetition." As athletes perform a successful behavior repeatedly, they improve their chances of achieving excellence.

In many religious traditions, there are examples of repetitive prayer leading to increased confidence and desired outcomes. As we speak our prayers out loud and focus on the completed goal, whether it is a healthy body, increased financial wealth, harmonious relationships, happiness, etc., we stop the fearful mind from having any power to attract what we don't want and we enable our desires to manifest. As we focus our attention on something that we desire, our subconscious will illuminate evidence so that we notice its presence. One of my favorite new thought teachers from the 1920s, Florence Scovel Shinn, said, "We cannot always control our thoughts, but we can control our words, and repetition impresses the subconscious, and we are then master of the situation." Repetitive prayer or spiritual chanting can drown out negative thoughts and take us to a peaceful place where we are still and receptive to our ultimate spiritual advisor. As we repetitively describe a desired outcome and have confidence that our spiritual partner can help us to achieve it, we are conditioning ourselves to realize more answers to our prayers. We will recognize more opportunities to take steps to achieve what we desire.

Business people establish a course for their desired growth, profitability, sales, efficiency, and other areas within their businesses. Leaders often convey the plan for successful outcomes to their teams. Management gathers employees together to communicate the projected goals. Many even post these goals throughout the company and talk about them regularly so that all employees are aware of the goals for their departments. Zig Ziglar, one of the greatest business and motivational speakers, said, "Repetition is the mother of learning, the father of action, which makes it the architect of accomplishment." I agree! As we keep our goals at the forefront of our thoughts, we're likely to see opportunities to achieve them.

In one of my recent healthcare ventures, we employed a number of entry level implementation specialists. These workers traveled the country assisting our project managers to install software and equipment to automate hospital pharmacies. Pete,[1] one of the implementation specialists, used repetition as a key to his success. Each day he would use his daily success practice to describe his goal with gratitude in becoming the best that he could be in his job. While on site with a supervising project manager, Pete felt intuitively guided to ask to do more of the implementation, and subsequently thought of innovative ways to perform his tasks. His project manager was impressed.

Several months later, Pete volunteered to work on the biggest projects and continued to practice what he was learning. Pete not only wanted to do well in his assigned work, but he wanted to create new solutions to help the company and its customers succeed in their missions. He used his daily practice to gratefully describe what his life would be like as he served his coworkers, company, and customers in valuable ways. He followed the intuitive guidance that he received.

One day, Pete had a strong intuitive thought to ask his boss if he could take customer service calls in the middle of the night so that he could practice problem solving while helping more customers. As he learned more about the common problems that customers were having, he received strong intuitive ideas about solutions. He discussed these with his boss and got approval to develop ways in which

---

1   All of the names in this book have been changed to protect privacy.

he could train customers differently during the implementation process to prevent the same types of problems in their organizations. This reduced the number of customer service calls and resulted in happier customers.

Pete's efforts didn't go unnoticed by his bosses and it wasn't long before Pete was promoted to a project manager position, earning a raise of more than $25,000 per year. All of this happened for Pete in less than two years. Pete's repetitive daily practice combined with following his CSO's intuitive directions helped him to reach his goals for himself, his customers, coworkers, and company. It allowed him to achieve a higher level of success sooner than he expected. You can use your daily practice and partnership with the CSO to experience greater levels of success, too!

According to British-based researchers Michael J. Howe, Jane W. Davidson, and John A. Sluboda in their published study, *Innate Talents; Reality or Myth*, "Large amounts of regular practice were found to be essential for excelling." They further indicated that the most successful people in any field are those who devote the most hours to what the researchers call "deliberate practice" rather than to what has been described as innate talents.

This is great news! As you incorporate gratitude with a regular deliberate daily practice, you will begin to excel at achieving more of your goals. In the daily practice system that I will describe more fully in this book, I show examples of how it has helped people to achieve personal and professional success. Abundance, prosperity, happiness, health, harmonious relationships, and more are available to anyone who is willing to set aside time for their daily practice and follow directions from their new partner as the CSO.

It's my belief that as we master the use of spiritual tools and rely more on the intelligent source of our intuition as our CSO to guide us, we can experience extraordinary events as miracles with greater frequency so that they become typical occurrences in our lives. Wouldn't you love that? It's possible! I'm so thrilled that you're beginning today to create the life that you desire.

The Daily Success System

The daily practice that is part of the system for success includes seven simple steps. This practice requires you to spend 30 minutes each morning with your spiritual partner or CSO to do the first four steps. Throughout the day, you will do steps five and six as you interact with your CSO. You'll recognize and follow intuitive messages, or you'll ask for clarification of additional leads on your path to achieve your goals. In the evening, you will do step seven as you give forth anything within you that is taking up room and not benefiting you, so that you have more room available to receive more of the good things that you desire.

Let's break this down into the morning, daytime, and evening practice.

The Morning Practice

Each morning, you will hold a 30-minute meeting with your CSO to review your goals in every area of your life: your health, your finances, your relationships, your work or use of skills and talents, your recreation, and your spiritual connection. Your morning meeting with your CSO should happen first thing when you wake up. I've found that it's important not to look at any mobile device or let the world's happenings take my attention before I hold my meetings. Let your family know that this time is important to you and to not disturb you during your morning meeting time.

Starting your morning by reviewing your goals with your new partner will set the tone for your day and lay a foundation of peace that will be evident no matter what comes up. American artist and New Thought spiritual teacher Florence Scovel Shinn tells us, "If you don't run your subconscious mind yourself, someone else will run it for you." As you become focused and proclaim gratitude for desired outcomes that you want to experience, you will train your brain to look for possibilities to achieve what you want and you'll feel happier and more energized throughout your day. If you allow others to program your attention, you'll see more evidence of the things *they* feel are important.

To demonstrate to yourself that you are serious about achieving your goals, it's helpful to create a comfortable space in your home (that is not your bed) to hold your daily planning meeting. It's perfectly fine to wear your pajamas to the meeting, but get out of bed and move to a different part of your home. A couch, comfortable chair, or dining room table are all appropriate places to hold your meeting. You will need a few tools to use during your meeting: an uplifting book with stories that put you into a receptive mood, a journal or notebook to write in, and a pen or pencil.

Take your meeting time seriously and commit to attending with your new partner every day in order to realize the greatest benefit.

Think of this meeting with your CSO as you would a meeting with the most successful advisor that you can imagine. Often, when I ask people to describe the most successful person that they can imagine—whose advice they would highly value—I hear names like Bill Gates, Gandhi, Oprah Winfrey, Walt Disney, Albert Einstein, Indra Nooyi, Mother Theresa, Nelson Mandela, and similar powerful people from the past or present.

I want to ask you the same question. Who is one person, living or not, that you believe could give you the most valuable advice to help you achieve what you want in life? Now, imagine that this person has agreed to meet with you every morning to go over your goals and give you advice throughout the day to achieve them. After receiving their advice, you could choose to take the action they suggest, or you could ask for more information. They would provide additional clarification if requested, and eventually you would feel comfortable taking the steps they recommend to achieve your goals. My question to you is this: would you agree to meet with that person every morning? Most people would say "yes."

You should treat your morning practice meeting and partnership with your CSO the same way. The all-knowing power of the universe has access to information that is beyond what your rational mind can imagine. This information can be helpful in guiding you in miraculous ways to achieve all that you desire, require, and more with greater ease and joy. Everyone can choose to access this source of intelligence through their partner, the CSO. Make a commitment to meet with your new partner each day.

Each morning, set aside 30 minutes for your meeting to perform the first four steps of the daily practice. Let's go over those right now.

Step 1: Read Something Inspirational

Step 1 requires you to read something inspirational and uplifting for five to ten minutes. I find that short stories about ordinary people having extraordinary accomplishments as a result of using a spiritual system for success are great for this step. It makes me believe that it's possible for me to have similar kinds of successes. Any book that inspires you is fine for this step.

As I started to read about other people's success and experience success for myself, I developed more confidence that all things that I desired were possible if I continued to use gratitude with my daily success practice. I got a chance to test this on a new level when I was asked by my clients to write a book based on the spiritual coaching I'd been providing for years.

My first thought was that I couldn't write a book because I wasn't trained to be a writer. I had a strong belief that I couldn't compare to the brilliant authors whose books I loved to read like James Allen, Catherine Ponder, Jack Canfield, Emma Curtis Hopkins, Napoleon Hill, Jane Austen, Michael Gerber, Malcolm Gladwell, Eckhart Tolle, and more. To help shift my beliefs, I started to read uplifting stories about some of these authors and their journeys to success. I also read other stories about spiritual guidance and intervention as part of achieving seeming impossible goals.

As my confidence grew, I created a goal to be a published author and I used gratitude as part of my daily practice system to describe what I desired as my outcome. The CSO provided me with tremendous intuitive insights and directions to take steps to achieve my goal, and my book, *The Path to Wealth*: *Seven Spiritual Steps for Financial Abundance*, was published in 2015.

No matter what your goal is, use the daily practice to make what you desire familiar and welcome in your thinking. Read about the journeys of others who have achieved the success that you desire so that you can begin to shift your beliefs to those of possibility. Become familiar with stories about others who relied on the all-knowing power of the universe to guide them to achieving their goals. As you recognize that you can experience this kind of achievement, you will begin to notice more opportunities and guidance from your CSO which will allow you to take action on the path to your own success.

I've included some suggested books that you can read for this part of your daily meeting in the Appendix of this book, but any book that inspires you and helps you believe that it's possible to achieve the life you desire is perfect for this step.

Step 2: Write a Gratitude Letter

Step 2 involves writing a letter to your CSO to express what you're grateful for that you have now, and what you want to achieve as your goals. It's important to word your goals with gratitude—as though you've already achieved them—with the outcomes that you desire. This will enable your subconscious and your CSO's intuitive messages to guide you to their completion.

A man I know once told me that he wanted a new job. As we discussed the outcome of his goal, we discovered that he didn't necessarily want a new job. What he really wanted was to have satisfying work, to feel appreciated, and to be paid more. He wrote down his completed goal each day as part of his CSO gratitude letter: "Thank you, CSO, that I use my remarkable skills and talents in satisfying and fulfilling ways. I am appreciated and valued by my company, coworkers, and customers and am rewarded with more than $_____ of dollars per year in income. I love my work."

Over the next several weeks, the man acted on intuitive and subconscious messages to use his talents in satisfying ways. As he followed guidance from his CSO to help his coworkers and customers solve problems, he felt their appreciation for him grow. He began to enjoy his work much more. Not long after this, his boss called him into her office and remarked that the management team had noticed that his attitude had been more positive and that his work had improved. When he was asked what changed, he mentioned that he liked his work and enjoyed helping his customers and company to succeed. His boss promoted him a week later and gave him a raise equal to the amount of money that he had established as his goal. He got a new job with higher pay without having to leave his current company. He felt more appreciated in the process. Writing out his gratitude letter with his properly worded, completed goal enabled his CSO to guide him to achieving the outcomes he desired.

Dr. Gail Matthews, a psychology professor at the Dominican University in California, presented findings of her study on goal setting at the May 2015 Ninth Annual International Conference of the Psychology Research Unit of Athens Institute for Education and Research (ATINER). In her study, Dr. Matthews gathered 267 people and divided the participants into groups according to who wrote down their goals and dreams and who didn't. Her groups were comprised randomly of men and women from all over the world and from all walks of life, including entrepreneurs, educators, healthcare professionals, artists, lawyers, and bankers. Dr. Matthews discovered through her research that people become 42 percent more likely to achieve their goals and dreams simply by writing them down on a regular basis. Writing down your goals in your daily CSO gratitude letter will help you achieve more of what you desire.

The following is an outline of a gratitude letter format that you can use for Step 2 each day:

- **Opening:** Dear CSO, (or whatever you name your source of intuition as your spiritual partner).

- **Part 1:** Write out gratitude statements for what you have now. "Thank you, CSO, for my [the things that you have now]."

- **Part 2:** Write out gratitude statements for what you want, but word them as though you have already achieved them. "Thank you, CSO, for my [the things that you want, worded as though you already have them]."

- **Part 3:** Acknowledge that your CSO is your ultimate advisor, which is part of the all-knowing power of the universe. "Thank you, CSO, for being the ultimate advisor who guides me to achieve all that I desire, require, and more." Proclaim the power that the ultimate advisor represents for you.

- **Part 4:** State that you release what you just wrote to the universe and that you recognize that it is now done. "I now release these words to the universe and am confident and grateful that it is all done."

- **Closing:** Close your letter as you would normally, e.g., "With love and gratitude," or "Your friend," and sign your name.

I've included a sample of one of my gratitude letters in the Appendix for you to refer to. Please note, it's important to use your own words that create excitement within you in your CSO gratitude letter.

Writing down your goals as if they are complete in your gratitude letter each day is part of the system for success that will enable your subconscious and your CSO to point out opportunities to achieve them sooner. If you need additional help to create powerful goal attainment statements, please consider using the *Goal Planning Guidebook* and companion audio CD available at www.bizzultz.com/store. I've also listed some elements from the Guidebook later in this book and in the Appendix to help you create powerful goal statements of your own.

Step 3: Speak with Emotion

Step 3 is to speak what you wrote out loud for up to five minutes. Any school teacher will tell you that reading something out loud anchors the meaning more fully within you. Read your letter out loud with emotion to magnetize yourself to receiving your desires.

New research by Professor Victor Boucher of the University of Montreal, published in *Consciousness and Cognition* (November 2015, pages 139–146), found that speaking information out loud can help people retain it better in their memory. Boucher said, "The simple fact of articulating without making a sound creates a sensorimotor link that increases our ability to remember, but if it is related to the functionality of speech, we remember even more." Hearing yourself speak your gratitude letter out loud will help you remember and keep your goals at the forefront of your thoughts throughout the day. You will notice more possibilities that are in line with your spoken goals.

As an added benefit, speaking your letter out loud serves as a nice self-check to confirm whether you're using the right words to describe your completed goals with gratitude.

For example, I know a saleswoman who would often say things like, "I really hope that I'm not late for my appointment with ABC Company on Tuesday. They are a huge potential customer, and I don't want them to buy from my competitor." Do you see anything out of the ordinary in this statement? Perhaps not, since many of us have learned to speak like this. We spend time talking about what we *don't* want as a normal part of our speech. Then we're surprised when exactly what we didn't want happens. In this example, the saleswoman is more likely to be late for her appointment with ABC Company since that's what she's focused on, and she may lose the sale to one of her competitors. Her subconscious recognizes that she's focused on being late and her competitor winning out. Accordingly, she may act in a way that makes those statements come true. This is not what she really wants to happen.

In Step 3 of her morning practice, she would ideally hear herself say those words out loud and it would become clear they need to be changed to more powerful goal statements. She might revise her goal to be, "I am so grateful to be on time or early for all of my appointments. I'm excited to sell our products to customers who receive great value in return." With statements like these, her subconscious and intuitive messages will show up in more obvious ways to help make those statements true. She might get a strong, unexpected thought to check the traffic report before she decides on a route to the appointment and avoid a terrible jam. She may feel an intuitive nudge to get ready sooner than she normally does so that she can leave earlier. She might receive an email or phone call that gives her insight into her customer's needs so that her presentation can be designed to be more valuable.

Speak your words out loud while describing your completed goals with gratitude in order to anchor the meaning more fully within you. This will help you notice more possibilities all day long.

Step 4: Imagine Experiencing Your Good

Finally, Step 4 involves your imagination. In your mind, see yourself as having completed one or two of your goals, for up to five minutes. This is a technique that many professional athletes, musicians, and business people use to succeed. Imagine yourself in your healthy body, with a big bank account, in harmonious relationships with others, with satisfying work, and enjoying recreation while living a balanced life. See in your mind and feel in your body all aspects of your completed goals. Mentally picture the answers to questions about your future life: who are you with, what are you doing, how do you feel, where are you, what surrounds you, what do you have, etc.

Successful athletes use this technique as part of their daily training routine. Nicole Detling, a sports psychologist with the United States Olympics, said, "The more an athlete can image the entire package, the better it's going to be. This is, more than ever, a multisensory endeavor, which is why the term 'imagery' is now often preferred to visualization." Emily Cook, the veteran American Olympic aerialist said, "Visualization, for me, doesn't take in all the senses. You have to smell it. You have to hear it. You have to feel it—everything."

Whatever your goal is, mentally see and feel what it's like to live the outcome of having it first. Then, your subconscious and CSO's intuitive messages will illuminate more possibilities to help you achieve it.

An added bonus of imagining your completed goal is that you'll be able to describe the images the next day in your gratitude letter with greater detail and emotion to make them seem more real.

Using these four steps each day as part of your system for success will lay the foundation for you to be happier and more peaceful throughout the day. You will feel lighter and become aware of more possibilities for taking steps to achieve your goals with greater ease and joy.

A number of scientific studies over the years have shown that performing simple gratitude exercises, like writing letters of thanks or speaking gratitude statements out loud, can bring a range of benefits that include feelings of improved well-being and reduced depression. These benefits can remain with us long after we've completed the exercises.

In the study, "The effects of gratitude expression on neural activity," published in the March 2016 *NeuroImage Journal* (pages 1–432), researchers Prathik Kini, Joel Wong, Sydney McInnis, Nicole Gabana, and Joshua W. Brown help us to understand why gratitude exercises have an effect. The results of the study show that even months after simple gratitude exercises and tasks, people's brains are still wired to feel thankful. The study suggests that the more you practice gratitude, the more attuned you are to it and the more you can enjoy its psychological benefits. Not only will you feel an improved sense of well-being, but your expressions of gratitude as part of your system for success will help you to stay in a receptive state in order to achieve more of the experiences that you desire with less of the work.

Summary of the Morning Practice

Commit to your morning meetings with your CSO each day for a minimum of 30 days. This will help you create a new gratitude habit so that you achieve more of your goals with greater ease. You will prove to yourself that miracles as "extremely outstanding or unusual events" manifest for you more often, in easier ways. You'll be convinced that success is not a secret, it's a system. As you master this system, you'll find that extremely outstanding events will become typical—even normal—to you.

While using your words, thoughts, and emotions to describe what you want instead of what you don't want, you will start to notice guidance from your CSO more often and in more obvious ways toward the actions that will enable you to achieve what you desire.

The four steps in the morning practice are part of a routine that will prime your brain for success. As you meet with your CSO each day, you will make your realized goals more familiar to you and you'll increase your belief that it's possible for you to have them. As Muhammad Ali, one of the greatest athletes of all time, said, "It's the repetition of affirmations that leads to belief. And once that belief becomes a deep conviction, things begin to happen."

Repeat these four steps every morning, and your conviction will grow. Good things will begin to happen for you, too.

The following is a suggested meeting agenda for your CSO meeting that begins at 6:00 a.m.:

The CSO Meeting Agenda

Date: _____. The CSO and I attended the meeting.

6:00 a.m.

Step 1: Read something spiritual and uplifting to get into a receptive mood.

I read: _____

6:10 a.m.

Step 2: Write out gratitude statements in a letter to the CSO. Include those things that I am grateful for that I have now, and those that I want as though they are already manifest in my life. (Use a notebook or a journal for your daily CSO letter.)

6:20 a.m.

Step 3: Speak as I read my letter out loud with emotion.

6:25 a.m.

Step 4: Imagine, think about, and feel grateful for all that I've listed as my desires, as though I already have them. What does it feel like to have them now? How do I look having those things or experiences?

Exercise

Take a few minutes to think of just one of your goals. Now use the following guide to practice the morning meeting outline for that goal:

Step 1: Read Something Inspirational

Read the following short story:

> I committed to set the alarm to wake up for my goal planning meeting each morning. It was tough for the first few days, but later in the week I found that I woke up before my alarm and had more energy throughout the day. One of my goals was to have good relationships with my family members. We had found ourselves in a cycle of finding fault with one another and spending more time on work, school, and other activities. I missed having the close and easy relationship that we had in the past. Each day, my goals would include statements like, "Thank you, CSO, that I love everyone and everyone loves me. I love myself. I bless everyone and everyone blesses me. I bless myself. I forgive everyone and everyone forgives me. I forgive myself. I'm so grateful that I have harmonious, peaceful and happy relationships with all of my family, my friends, and my coworkers. I love that we treat each other with respect and enjoy each other's company." I continued with the same goal, switching up the words a bit to describe my joy for the completed goal more fully. After three weeks,

my son came home with great news about his team being invited to travel to a baseball tournament near the beach. I mentioned this to my friend who said that her sister owned a property near the beach, and she checked to see if our family could use it. The sister agreed and wouldn't accept any payment for it. I requested some vacation time from my boss, which he approved, and he gave me several free meal certificates for his friend's restaurant near where we would be staying. Our family got to spend a whole week together enjoying each other in the close and joyfully easy way that I had been describing in my CSO meeting. And, we were given a beautiful beach home to use and free meals at a great restaurant. I'm so grateful to my CSO for orchestrating this wonderful vacation for me and my family.

Step 2: Write a Gratitude Letter

Opening: e.g., "Dear CSO," or whatever you name your source of intuition as your spiritual partner.

Part 1: Write out gratitude statements for what you have now, e.g., "Thank you, CSO, for my [list a few things that you have now]."

_____

_____

_____

_____

Part 2: Write out gratitude statements for what you want, but word them as though you have already achieved them, e.g., "Thank you, CSO, for my [the goal that you want, worded as though you have already received it with gratitude]."

_____

_____

_____

_____

Part 3: Acknowledge that your CSO is your ultimate advisor, which is part of the all-knowing power of the universe, e.g., "Thank you, CSO, for being the ultimate advisor who guides me to achieve all that I desire, require, and more." Proclaim the power that the ultimate advisor represents for you.

_____

_____

_____

_____

Part 4: State that you release what you just wrote to the universe and that you recognize that it is now done, e.g., "I now release these words to the universe and am confident and grateful that it is all done."

_____

_____

_____

_____

Closing: Close your letter as you would normally, e.g., "With love and gratitude," or "Your friend," and sign your name.

_____

_____

Step 3: Speak the Letter Out Loud

Read what you wrote above out loud to anchor the meaning within you. Listen to your words and make any changes necessary to make them more meaningful to you.

Step 4: Imagine Your Goal Completed

Close your eyes. In your mind, imagine your entire surroundings. Feel and see your experience after you've achieved your desired goal. If you struggle with imagery, get pictures that represent your completed goal. Look at them briefly, then close your eyes to see yourself in the pictures. Once you're able to do that, you will begin to imagine more details and feelings that are in line with your completed goal.

How do you feel after doing the exercise above? In workshops that I present around the country, I ask participants the same question. The words that they use include "happy," "energized," "hopeful," "clarity," "peaceful," and other positive descriptions. I hope that is your experience as well.

Set Your Intention for the Morning Practice

Important elements of your morning practice include consistency and gratitude. Set the alarm to wake up in time to hold your meeting every morning with your CSO. Many people tell me that after a few days, they wake up before the alarm goes off and are excited about attending their meeting. As mentioned earlier, studies have shown that gratitude practices have long-lasting beneficial effects. With the benefits of increased energy and vitality, you will find that you're more productive and have an increased sense of peace and happiness all day long. You deserve to have the success that you desire, and the morning gratitude routine will help you achieve that with greater ease and joy along the way.

To receive the greatest benefit from any relationship, the partners need to spend time getting to know each other and building a high level of trust. Have you ever heard the phone ring and you knew who it was before you answered? If that has happened for you, most likely you have a close relationship with the caller. The same is true in building your relationship with your CSO. Your morning meeting helps you to get to know your CSO and to build a level of trust in your partnership. As your relationship strengthens, it will become easier for you to recognize when your CSO is providing you with intuitive messages and pointing out opportunities.

There are a few times when I have to get up quite early and am short on time before I have to leave for the airport or go to another commitment. When that happens, I do one of two things: I pack up my CSO meeting materials and hold my meeting on the plane, or I write a short thank you note to my CSO for my wonderful life before I leave for my event. Even that short note supports my role in the partnership. You can hold a shorter meeting if necessary on occasion and still support your valuable relationship with your CSO. Once you're back to your normal routine, hold your morning meetings as outlined in the morning practice.

Remember, your morning CSO meeting is part of a system for success, an opportunity for you to achieve more of your desires with less of the work. Consistency, repetition, and gratitude are the keys. Make sure that you hold your meeting every morning to get the greatest benefit so that you can achieve the happy, healthy, prosperous, and free life that you desire.

The Daytime Practice

Once you complete your morning meeting with your CSO, you will feel more energized and excited to begin your normal daily activities and work. Throughout the day, you will practice Steps 5 and 6 of your daily system for success. As you move through your day, you will think about your completed goals and receive intuitive messages from your CSO that guide and direct you to take action.

When you receive an intuitive message, you have a choice to make: take an action step, or, if you need additional clarification, ask for another lead. The second option is very simple to do. When you are first learning to do it, I want you to tilt your head slightly up and say, "CSO, I need another lead." That's all you have to do. You can ask for as many confirming leads as you want to. What you are not allowed to do anymore is nothing.

Albert Einstein said that we each have an intuitive mind and a rational mind. A popular quote attributed to Einstein says, "The intuitive mind is a sacred gift, and the rational mind is a faithful servant. We've created a society that honors the servant and has forgotten the gift." Today, more than ever, we are a society that honors the rational mind. When we have a question about anything, what do we do? We Google it! We figure out ways to get more information and then we analyze, measure, and evaluate the information. We consider every possible step that we can take and every possible outcome that could happen as a result. Only if we like the outcome possibilities, do we act. Otherwise, we do nothing. This is not a system for success.

If you feel unsure about an intuitive lead that you have received, just ask for another lead and wait until you get one before taking action. While waiting, your rational mind may try to talk you out of taking a step or listening to your CSO. This is not uncommon. Don't let it deter you. Continue to wait for a lead from your CSO.

I know a woman I will call Janice, who needed to sell a property in another country that she had rented out for over ten years. Upon seeing the property after the renters moved, Janice fell into deep despair. The home had not been taken care of and was in need of extensive cleaning and repair. Since she hadn't lived in the community for over 15 years, she didn't know whom to contact to get help. Over the next few days, Janice used her morning practice and meeting with her CSO to describe an easy and affordable solution. She created goal statements that described her completed goals and desired outcomes with gratitude: "Thank you, CSO, that I easily and joyfully have available to me the right resources and time to prepare my home for sale. I'm grateful that the right buyers are brought to me at the right time to purchase my beautiful home for the right price and that they enjoy living there immensely. All of this unfolds easily and joyfully without delay."

Within a few days, the woman had a strong thought to go to a taco bar for lunch. That didn't make any sense to her since she didn't normally eat tacos and her rational mind communicated to her through her thoughts that this was a terrible idea. Instead of listening to her rational mind and doing nothing, she figuratively stomped her foot and said, "CSO, if this lead is from you, give me another lead to confirm it." Then she went back to cleaning up. Two days later, she had the same thought again: Go to the taco bar for lunch. So she did.

After walking through the door and looking at the menu board, someone called her name. It was an old friend that remembered when she and her husband lived there over 15 years ago. As they had lunch together, Janice explained why she was in town. This man said that he was a contractor and had a one-week break between jobs. He told her that he could prepare her house for sale for a fraction of the cost of his normal rate and offered to help. She accepted and quietly thanked her CSO for the lead.

Before they finished lunch, Janice asked the man if he had been to the taco bar a couple days before for lunch. He replied that he had. She smiled and quietly thanked her CSO for being such a wonderful partner. I'm happy to report that the repairs were completed within Janice's budget and her home was sold quickly for a fair price. Everyone included in the transaction was happy.

Your morning planning meeting will help you keep your goals at the forefront of your thoughts, so that you can notice messages from your CSO throughout the day to guide you to achieving your desires. When you receive an intuitive lead from your CSO, either take action or ask for another lead. Most people have already proved how revisiting a goal often can be effective.

Think about the last time that you purchased a car. If you're like most people, when buying a car you think about the different models that you like, talk to friends and family about them, search for reviews, and maybe take a test drive to narrow down your selection to one that you like. You imagine all aspects of owning that particular car. Don't you then start to notice that car driving around everywhere? You never noticed it before it was a goal. You now start to notice it because you've kept the goal at the forefront of your thoughts and used repetition to create the belief that it's possible for you to have what you desire. When that happens, your subconscious filters all of the data coming at you to help you notice that car. Your CSO will then add intuitive messages to direct your actions so that you can own your new car. This simple system for success can be used for all of your goals, including perfect work, health, relationships, recreation, finances, and spiritual connection.

Steps 5 and 6 of the daytime practice happen throughout the day. They include forming your expectations, noticing leads, celebrating, and accumulating proof that your partnership is working.

Step 5: Expect Leads and Follow Directions

Step 5 is to expect and watch for leads, and follow the directions provided by your CSO. Throughout the day, you will be on constant lookout for intuitive messages and directions from your CSO to take some sort of action, like the strong thought that Janice had to go to the taco bar.

There is power in positive expectation. In a 2007 research study conducted by Harvard's Alia J. Crum and Ellen J. Langer, called "Mind-set matters: Exercise and the placebo effect" published in *Psychological Science* (vol 18, no. 2: pages 165-171), we learn that positive expectations have an effect on your health. In the study, 84 female room attendants working in seven different hotels were measured on physiological health variables affected by exercise. Those in the informed group were told that the hotel cleaning work they do is good exercise and is in accordance with the Surgeon General's recommendations for an active lifestyle. They were shown how their work was beneficial exercise for their bodies. Subjects in the control group were not given this information. Four weeks after the intervention, the informed group perceived themselves to be getting significantly more exercise than before. As a result, compared with the control group, they showed a decrease in weight, blood pressure, body fat, waist-to-hip ratio, and body mass index. Because they positively expected their work to be healthy and beneficial to them, they were able to realize measurable positive effects from it.

In the study, "Optimism and Cause-Specific Mortality: A Prospective Cohort Study," published in the January 2017 issue of the *American Journal of Epidemiology*, postdoctoral research fellow and co-lead author Kaitlin Hagan wrote, "Previous studies have shown that optimism can be altered with relatively uncomplicated and low-cost interventions—even something as simple as having people write down and think about the best possible outcomes for various areas of their lives, such as careers or friendships. Encouraging use of these interventions could be an innovative way to enhance health in the future." The simple daily practice for success combined with positive expectations for best possible outcomes will help you live an enhanced, healthier, and more successful life.

I'm often asked, "What is an intuitive lead and how do I notice it?" Leads can show up as a strong thought to contact someone, like the strong thought about my sister that led me to stop by her office. That was a lifesaving lead that enabled me to experience my completed goal for good health. Or you might get an idea to go somewhere or do something, like the taco bar moment. You may have a feeling in your gut or heart that is trying to tell you something, like Pete's intuitive feeling to take customer service calls for our company which led him to getting a promotion and raise. Or, you might see a sign or hear something from another person that resonates with you.

In one of my previous healthcare companies, I had asked my CSO for a lead about whether my company should do business with a $5.5 billion company located in San Diego which wanted to resell our products and services to their customers. Although I had received what most people would call definite and obvious leads, I kept asking for more leads because I was still unsure and uneasy about doing business with such a large company. On my way to work one morning, I noticed a billboard that I hadn't seen before. It said, "Your fortune will be made in San Diego." I started to laugh—my CSO has a sense of humor. I don't know how long that billboard had been up or how many times I had driven by without noticing it. That day, my CSO illuminated it as my lead to take action, so I did. I met with the San Diego company and I felt comfortable creating an agreement with them that resulted in a great relationship which lasted several years and was worth millions of dollars for both companies. We were able to serve our customers and employees in more valuable ways, and all of us benefited from the relationship.

As you expect and watch for leads, more intuitive directions will show up. When you get an intuitive lead, either take the step or ask for another lead. You can ask for as many leads as you want. Remember, you're no longer allowed to only take direction from your rational mind and do nothing.

I have a friend who said that she used her daily CSO meeting to describe a goal to take her daughter on a trip to California for spring break. She used her words to describe a fun and luxurious trip for a lower price than her budget allowed. She bought the plane tickets and contacted a friend who had said that she could use his vacation rental anytime. Unfortunately, her friend had just rented out his unit for the time that she was planning to be there. She was discouraged, but continued with her morning practice and affirmed "Thank you, CSO, that my daughter and I have a great, luxurious trip within my budget." A few days later, she had a strong hunch that she should book a room at a specific hotel. She looked at the hotel online, and the rooms cost over $100 more per night than she wanted to spend. That made her nervous, so she asked the CSO for another lead and kept up with her daily practice. Three days later, she received an email from the same hotel chain, offering a discount if she made a reservation that day. She made a reservation for the same hotel at $150 less per night than she had found earlier in the week. Her cost for the room was $50 less per night than her budget allowed. She was so grateful, and knew that the lead to stay at that hotel was from her CSO to help her to have a luxurious vacation within her budget. She and her daughter had a great time!

I believe that the hunch provided by her CSO about the hotel and her request for another lead helped her to notice, in the midst of dozens of other emails, the one with the advertisement for the hotel discount. Once she saw it, she felt comfortable in taking action. This can happen for you, too!

When you get an intuitive lead as a strong thought, a feeling in your gut or heart, a message from someone that resonates with you, or a sign that you feel is providing some direction, take the action step or ask for another lead. You can ask for as many leads as you need. The only rule is you're not allowed to do nothing.

Step 6: Celebrate and Note Demonstrations

Step 6 of the daytime practice is to celebrate and note demonstrations. This happens after you get a lead and take a step. It's important to celebrate even if you haven't reached your final goal. This becomes your proof that the partnership with your CSO is working—and it's really fun.

My friend contacted her celebration partner after she took a step and booked the discounted hotel room. She took action and celebrated. She also noted what happened in a small notebook.

I want you to think of at least one person to have as your celebration partner and how you'll contact each other. Get in touch with that person today and let them know that you'd like to celebrate with them when good things happen for each of you. Decide how you'll reach each other to celebrate—on the phone, in person, or via the internet. One of my celebration partners is in Louisiana. We text the word "celebrate" to each other and reply with times that we are available for a call to talk about what leads we received and the steps that we took.

Fill in the following as your commitment to celebrate with a partner:

My celebration partner is:

_____

To contact my celebration partner, I will:

_____

If you need additional celebration partners, consider joining our private Facebook group. People from around the world participate to celebrate with each other. Send a note to csogroup@bizzultz.com if you'd like to join us.

Celebrating helps you to recognize that your partnership with your CSO is working. It keeps you tuned up and happy so that you can notice more leads that provide more guidance along the way to achieving your goals. Using scientific research provided by

UC Berkley's Greater Good Science Center, the non-profit *Project Happiness* reports, "Only in recent years has research turned its focus on how happiness can be sustained and increased. Science has now confirmed that with certain practices we can change the neural pathways of our brain. Happiness is a set of skills we can learn through practice." Celebrating and gratitude are part of a repetitive practice that makes us happy. As we repeat this behavior, we change neural pathways in our brain that are tied to strong beliefs and behaviors. I'll share more about the importance of beliefs and behaviors later in the book.

As we experience positive emotions more often, the dopamine released in our brains enables us to focus and see more possibilities to take action toward our goals. As we celebrate, we will recognize more opportunities and intuitive leads to guide our success more often.

Throughout the day, if you get a lead that you don't understand or you feel unsure about, just ask for another lead, as my friend who wanted the luxurious and affordable vacation did. You will get one. Eventually, you will feel confident enough to take the necessary steps and celebrate your success. After celebrating, be sure to note your demonstrations in a notebook that you keep with you. Simply write down the lead that you got and the step that you took even if you haven't reached your goal yet. Noting demonstrations builds up your proof that your partnership is working.

In an April 2014 study published in *Psychological Science,* called "The Pen is Mightier than the Keyboard," researchers Pam Mueller and Daniel Oppenheimer, of Princeton University and UCLA respectively, showed that taking notes by hand forces the brain to engage mentally. These efforts foster comprehension and retention.

As you note your demonstrations of acting on leads that you receive, you're engaging your brain to notice and value the proof that your partnership with your CSO is working.

Choose a small notebook or pad that you can keep in your handbag, backpack, car, or desk that you will use for noting your demonstrations. Record below where you'll keep your notebook.

I keep my notebook with me in my

_____ [location].

As you celebrate and note your demonstrations to build confidence in your partnership, you'll begin to expect and receive more leads in more obvious ways to help guide you to greater success.

For example, Larry wanted more money, but he said that he barely had enough income to pay his bills each month and couldn't see any possibility of having more. I asked Larry what his life would be like if he had more money. He said among other things, that he'd be able to give to and support his church. In many traditions, this is referred to as tithing. Larry didn't trust the prosperity principle of tithing, which I believe is based on the Law of Giving and Receiving—as you give, you will receive the same or more. I asked Larry if he'd like to prove this Law in a cheerful and easy way. I requested that he make a commitment to using the daily CSO practice and make giving to his church a goal. Larry reminded me that he barely had enough money to make ends meet now. I told him to leave the "how" to achieve his goal up to his CSO. As a first step, I asked that he give from unexpected income only until he felt some confidence. He gave $5 to his church as a demonstration of his commitment. Within a week of focusing on his goal to be a cheerful giver, he had proof to celebrate. He noted that he had received unexpected income of $50, and he gave $5 to his church. The following week, he continued with his daily goal practice and, one day, followed his dog on a different route in a park that they visit often. On the new route, he found a roll of money amounting to $325. He looked around for anyone that could have dropped it and didn't find anyone close by. He looked for people along the trail and in the parking lot to see if anyone was looking for the lost money. No one was. He thanked his CSO, celebrated and noted his demonstration. He gave $32.50 the following week to his church. After six months of proving the Law of Giving and Receiving, Larry decided to give from the after tax net amount of his paycheck, plus any unexpected income. A few months later, he received a 20% raise at his job and celebrated! The daily success practice can be used for any goal that you have for your life. Larry saw proof that his goal for supporting his church was being made manifest.

For the Law of Giving and Receiving, a key tip for activating this power is to give consistently and to expect to receive. Spiritual writer Catherine Ponder said it this way, "Giving is only one half of the Law of Increase. Receiving is the other half. We can give and give but we may unbalance the Law unless we also expect to receive." As you expect and watch for leads and take action, you will receive more of the desires of your heart with greater joy and satisfaction.

At this point I hope that you're convinced that success is not a secret, it's a system. As you get clear about your goals and expect and watch for intuitive and subconscious directions to achieve them, you'll feel more confident in taking the steps that the CSO provides to you. Expressing gratitude, celebrating, and noting your action steps support an increased level of confidence. This system is provable and repeatable once you get used to the process.

The Evening Practice

There's one final point that is important to receiving anything into your life, and that is that you actually have to create room to receive it. I want you to imagine a full bottle of water. If it is filled up to the brim, can you fit anything more into it? No, you have to remove some of the water to allow more to come in. The same is true with you. You have to make room within yourself to receive more of what you want. If you are filled up with anything that isn't of benefit to you, it will have to be removed so that you can receive what you desire.

Think about the last time that you were really angry or worried about something. When you're like that, can anyone have a conversation with you? They can't because you're not present—you're consumed with whatever or whomever you're upset with. Negative ideas, thoughts, and emotions take your attention, and you can't hear anyone else speak when you're in that state. Intuitive messages from your CSO can't get through, either. You're filled up; there is no room within you to receive anything more that you desire.

Step 7: Offer Gratitude and Forgiveness

Step 7 happens at night and will help you remove these negative emotions so that you have room to receive your desired goals. Step 7 has two parts, and can be done in your bed. If you have a partner or spouse that isn't doing the daily success practice, you may want to do this in your CSO meeting area so you don't disturb them.

The first part takes place as you're ready to go to sleep. You will recite gratitude statements out loud for anything that happened during the day that you're happy about. For example, I say things like, "Thank you, CSO, for the parking spots that I got in front today so I didn't have to get wet in the Seattle rain." Or, "Thank you for my annual physical report, which shows my great health." Go over your day in your mind and choose some things that happened which you are grateful for. There are tremendous benefits that you'll experience as a result of being grateful.

In a University of California Davis online feature article, "Gratitude is Good Medicine", published in November 2015, Robert A. Emmons, professor of psychology at UC Davis, said, "Clinical trials indicate that the practice of gratitude can have dramatic and lasting effects in a person's life. It can lower blood pressure, improve immune function, and facilitate more efficient sleep." In the April 2015 journal *Spirituality in Clinical Practice*, Paul J. Mills published the study, "A Grateful Heart is a Healthier Heart", which was conducted at the University of California San Diego's School of Medicine. Mills learned that when using a gratitude practice, his subjects "showed a better well-being, a less depressed mood, less fatigue, and they slept better." As you use gratitude before sleep as part of the daily success practice, you'll experience greater health benefits and a better quality of sleep.

The second part of Step 7 is to recite a general "giving forth" or forgiveness prayer to remove anything within you that is taking up room and not serving you, so that you have room to receive what you want. Go ahead and read the following prayer out loud:

> CSO, if there is anyone from my past or present that I need to forgive, whether I remember them or not, I now do so. I bless them, I love them, I forgive them, and I release them into your care, knowing that you will work with them in whatever way is best. And, if there is anyone from my past or present who needs to forgive me, including myself, they now do so, and we are all free to experience a higher and greater good in our lives.

Now, take a deep breath. How do you feel? It's important to note that you don't have to believe these words; they still work. This prayer said on a repetitive basis helps to remove anything that is taking up room within you that is not for your highest and greatest good. It puts it outside of you so that you have room available to receive what you desire in life. You will feel lighter and freer as you do Step 7 each night as part of your daily practice.

A research team led by Michelle Zheng of Erasmus University's Rotterdam School of Management studied the effects of forgiveness. In their article, "The Unburdening Effects of Forgiveness," (published January 2015 in *Social Psychological and Personality Science*), they concluded "The benefits of forgiveness may go beyond the constructive consequences that have been established in the psychological and health domains. Our research shows that forgivers perceive a less daunting world, and perform better on challenging physical tasks." They add, "A state of unforgiveness is like carrying a heavy burden—a burden that victims bring with them when they navigate the physical world. Forgiveness can lighten this burden." State the giving forth prayer each night, and it will work to lighten your burden and make room within you to receive more of what you desire in life.

If there is something more that you need to do regarding forgiveness, your CSO will guide you to take action. But for now, your only concern is to recite the prayer before sleep. Say the forgiveness prayer each night and you will feel lighter, sleep better, and be more able to take on challenging tasks with ease.

Please understand that the giving forth prayer does not condone what others may have done in the past. Many painful and unjust things have happened in the past, and this is not a blanket excuse for any of them. This part of the daily system for success is simply to help you personally—to get you to a calm place so that you can recognize and follow your CSO partner's leads and to make room within you to receive more of what you want in life. I want you to live the wonderful life that you design. Now, more than ever, you deserve to live a happy, healthy, safe, and prosperous life. To do so, you have to make room available within yourself to receive what you desire. Step 7 and the entire daily practice will help you do that.

As an added bonus, in the study "Neuroimaging of Forgivability," published in the 2005 *Forgiveness Handbook*, Dr. Tom Farrow, a clinical psychologist at the University of Sheffield, and his colleagues used magnetic resonance imaging (MRI) to study the effects of forgiveness on the brain. They learned that when a person is in the process of forgiving, activity in the frontal lobe of the brain increases. The frontal lobe is involved in problem solving, complex thought, and the complex functions of thinking and reasoning. Based on this research, is it possible that in forgiving you are actually becoming smarter? I believe that anything is possible. Recite the giving forth or forgiveness prayer each night before sleep, and it will help you experience greater peace as well as freeing up room within you that can be filled with more of the good things that you desire in life.

The Practice in Your Life

While we may have never met, I care about you and want you to live the life that you desire, require, and more. Using these seven simple steps on a daily basis will help you train your brain for success and enable subconscious and intuitive messages from your CSO to show up more often, in more obvious ways. These messages will direct you along a path to achieve your goals.

We all get to make choices about the things that are important to us. As you focus more on what you want to experience rather than what you don't, you'll start to notice more possibilities that are in line with your desires. Gratitude and repetition of your words, thoughts, and emotions are valuable tools in this success system. Make a commitment to use this simple daily system and witness seeming miracles manifest in your life.

I believe that this is a generous and abundant universe and that success is available for each and every person. I hope that you recognize that you can begin now to live a wonderful life. With the use of these tools, you can have the life of your dreams—filled with greater happiness, health, abundance, and more, with less work and more peace.

Section 2:

ACHIEVING GOALS

Unless we create specific goals that match our purpose in life and unless we keep a clear vision of these goals, we may eventually falter and fail.

— SIR JOHN MARKS TEMPLETON

Achieving goals is not difficult, but deciding exactly what you want as a goal can be a challenging task. Many of us are too vague in describing what we want, or we talk about what we don't want and are then surprised that we get more of it.

In one of my workshops—which I hold around the country—a retired woman said that her goal was to be spiritually creative. I asked her if I could use her as an example and turned to ask if anyone in the workshop could give her advice to achieve her goal. No one raised their hand because her goal was too vague. I asked the woman if she would take some time to imagine her life after she achieved her goal to be spiritually creative. I asked her to determine what happened to make her believe that she met her goal. Later in the workshop, the woman said that she had the answer.

She said that she would feel successful, prosperous, and happy. She said that she imagined that her artwork was for sale in a minimum of 15 locations, and that it would be on notecards and T-shirts for sale as well. She went on to say that she'd receive at least $3,000 per month in income from the use of her artistic talents and skills, and the best part would be that at least once a week someone would contact her to say that after having seen her artwork, they felt inspired to create their own.

I then asked the class if anyone could give her some advice. Several hands were raised. Someone knew a couple of restaurants that would hang her work for sale on consignment; another person referred her to an online company that creates notecards. Someone else knew of a manufacturer that would allow her to upload artwork to create custom, affordable T-shirts. The retired woman was amazed and recognized that if all of these people could give her valuable advice, then her CSO would easily be able to give her more as she incorporated her goals into her daily practice. Once she became clear on what the outcome of her goal would be, her CSO could guide and direct her to achieve it.

I heard from this woman six months later and was delighted to learn that she was successful in exhibiting her artwork for sale in restaurant and convention spaces. She also shared that she had been invited to a number of art shows in assisted-living communities to sell her artwork. Not only did she sell her work, but she was asked to put on art workshops for a fee, which brought joy and satisfaction into the lives of the residents. She had achieved her goal and more.

In her 2011 *Harvard Business Review* article, "Nine Things Successful People Do Differently," writer Heidi Grant states that being specific about goals should be at the top of the list. "Knowing exactly what you want to achieve keeps you motivated until you get there." Be sure that you describe your completed goals with gratitude, and include some details to enable your subconscious and your CSO to illuminate more possibilities for you to achieve them. A note of caution: Describe your completed goals with gratitude, not the steps or the "how" that you will take to get there. That's your CSO's job to determine.

Describing what you want as an outcome, rather than describing what you don't want, is also part of the system for success. Many of us have been trained over time to speak about what we don't want, all the while thinking that is the same as expressing what we desire. What we don't realize is how our brain, subconscious, and spiritual partner interpret the idea of "don't want".

According to Matthew B. James (MA, PhD) in his 2013 *Psychology Today* article titled, "Conscious of the Unconscious," the unconscious " . . . does not process negatives. The unconscious absorbs pictures rather than words. So if you say, 'I don't want to procrastinate,' the unconscious generates a picture of you procrastinating. Switching that picture from the negative to the positive takes an extra step. Better to tell your unconscious, 'Let's get to work!'" As you picture an outcome, you will see more evidence of it occurring. It's important that you describe and imagine what you want the outcome to be.

For example, a man I know said that one of his goals was for his Uncle Bob to stop causing problems at the family reunion. He said that he's had this goal for years, and at every reunion he noticed problems caused by his Uncle Bob. I pointed out that his subconscious wouldn't notice the idea of *not* wanting Uncle Bob to cause problems. What he'd most likely see evidence of is his Uncle Bob continuing to cause problems.

To understand his real goal, I asked him some questions about what his life would be like if Uncle Bob wasn't causing problems at the family reunion. He said:

- He'd have a fun time at the reunion.

- He would be happy and feel free to be in harmonious relationships with everyone.

- He would have great conversations with family members, and he would feel at peace.

Then I asked him to create some goal statements that used what he described as the outcome of his good experience. He came up with the following: "I'm so grateful that I have a really fun time at my family reunion, and enjoy having meaningful conversations with my relatives as we operate freely and in harmony and peace with each other. I am so happy that I'm a part of my family and I am grateful that we are able to be together."

With goal statements like that, the man may feel intuitively led to go outside to sit and visit with some relatives and completely miss Uncle Bob entering the room. If the man isn't looking for the problem, most likely there won't be one to witness. His goals were about his experience, not Uncle Bob's. I'm happy to report that he did experience a wonderful time at his latest family reunion and even enjoyed some time spent with his Uncle Bob.

Creating Powerful Goals

The daily success practice can assist you in receiving all that you desire, require, and more. But, it stands to reason that you need to be clear on what you desire and require first. It's important to have goals for each major area of your life, and you need to word them in such a way that enables your subconscious and the intuitive messages from your CSO to show up and be recognized.

The major areas of your life in which to focus your goals include your health, wealth and finances, fulfilling and satisfying use of your skills and talents (or work), harmonious relationships, recreation, spiritual connection, and your world. Outlined below are a few sections from my *Goal Planning Guidebook* to assist you in creating the right, most powerful goals for you to use. As you use your new goals each day as part of your system for success, your understanding will grow, and you'll notice more possibilities from your CSO to take steps along the path to achieve what you desire.

Health and Well-Being

Health is a topic that interests everyone. Many of us create goals for the size of our bodies, the movement through life without pain, and our longevity. Our health can be affected by factors such as our genetics, age, living conditions, physical activity, consumption of food, alcohol, and medications, emotional and mental disposition, and a number of others.

None of these factors can stop you from experiencing a healthy life if you decide that's what you want. This section is to help you define your healthy life and create goal statements to achieve it.

For example, a woman named Clare had grandparents, parents, and much older siblings who had all been diagnosed with diabetes. She had been told from a young age that she would also have diabetes because it was genetic. She didn't want to have that experience; she wanted to be healthy. So, she started using her daily success practice and created powerful goal statements: "I am so grateful that I am physically fit, trim, toned, and energetic in a perfectly healthy body that is free from pain and is easily able to go on hikes and walks with my family and friends. We have a great time!"

Each day Clare used her daily CSO meeting to write down her goal, read it out loud, and imagine being in the healthy body and lifestyle that she wanted. Within a few days, someone had mentioned a nutrition program that she could join to learn more about food and the ways in which it works with her body. Her gut instinct told her to sign up, so she did. In the waiting room at a subsequent appointment, Clare met a woman who introduced her to some new friends that liked to be outdoors. They invited her to walk, hike, and bike ride with them. Over the course of about four months, Clare found that she was living the healthy lifestyle that she imagined, and was more than 40 pounds lighter. Her doctor told her that her change in diet and activity would help to prevent any onset of diabetes. Intuition and her subconscious showed up through thoughts, gut feelings, and messages from other people to guide and direct her to her completed goal. You can have similar success with your goal!

To begin to create your goal statements, answer the following questions:

What is your description of the ideal, perfect health for you?

_____

_____

_____

_____

Describe what your life would be like after achieving your idea of perfect health. How do you feel? What are you doing? Who are you with? Where are you? How does achieving the goal affect others related to you: your company, your family, community, etc.?

_____

_____

_____

_____

Review your answers to these questions and begin to create goal attainment statements that include the outcome of having your achieved your goal with gratitude.

> **Example:** "I am so grateful that I have a healthy, fit, pain-free body that moves through life easily and always feels well rested. I feel beautiful in my clothes and enjoy spending time with my friends and family dancing, walking, skiing, and having fun with a great sense of freedom. I am more productive at work, and my energy easily lasts throughout the day. I love my healthy life."

_____

_____

_____

_____

Wealth and Finances

Money is a tool that can be available to each and every one of us in whatever measure we believe that we can achieve. To increase your financial wealth to a level that you haven't experienced before will require you to increase your belief that it's possible for you to have the new level of wealth. To do that, you need to create powerful goal-attainment statements to be used daily in your morning practice and recited throughout the day. You'll also need to read stories about and talk to others who have attained the level of wealth that you'd like to achieve. Making their journey familiar to you helps to strengthen a belief that it's possible for you to have the same level of wealth—and more.

For example, a man named Harold wanted to be a successful real estate agent in Southern California. He studied, got his license, and went to work for a broker. In the first eight months of his new job, the few clients that he worked with ran him ragged for very little money in commission. Harold couldn't rationally see how he could ever be a successful, well-paid agent with great clients, and started to consider other lines of work. But before he gave up, he committed to creating new goal statements and using them in the daily practice as part of his system for success.

He described his perfect clients and his desired amount of money with gratitude as though he had already achieved his goal. He also took steps to make the success that he wanted welcome by reading about the journeys of successful real estate agents and going to networking events to meet some of them and hear their stories. As he did his daily practice and met other successful agents over several months, his beliefs shifted. Harold started to believe that it was possible to experience the same kind of success. He didn't know how it was going to happen; he waited for his CSO to illuminate possibilities through intuitive leads.

A short time later, he got a strong thought to call surfing shops and corporations who had surfers as part of their executive teams to see if they'd like him to come in and speak for free about the risk-taking characteristics that surfing and business have in common. Since

Harold had been a competitive surfer earlier in his life, he learned how to take risks that could be applied to business situations with success. Several of the surf shops and corporations invited him to speak at their events. While there, he made new friends and contacts that resulted in a lot of new business referrals. I'm happy to say that Harold has surpassed his original financial goal and has now created new and larger ones.

As you become familiar with the desired good that you want, it will be easier for you to imagine having it. Using your daily practice with powerful goal statements and making what you want familiar to you will enable intuitive messages from your CSO to show up more often, in more obvious ways, to point the way for you to achieve your desires.

To begin to create your goal statements, answer the following questions:

> What is your description of a financially free and wealthy life?

_____

_____

_____

_____

Describe what your life would be like after achieving your idea of perfect wealth. How do you feel? What are you doing? Who are you with? Where are you? How does achieving the goal affect others related to you, your company, your family, community, etc.?

_____

_____

_____

_____

Review your answers to the questions above and begin to create goal attainment statements that include the outcome of having your achieved your goal with gratitude.

Example: "Thank you, CSO, that I am financially free and wealthy. I now have more than $_____ of income per year and feel satisfied, fulfilled, and happy at all times. I love using my skills and talents in remarkable ways to work towards the success of my company and employer, coworkers, customers, suppliers, and our world. I feel appreciated and valued at all times. I am so grateful that all that I desire and require for my living, giving, and entertainment expenses are easily and readily available to me without delay. I am at peace and live a wonderful and balanced life that is so very good."

_____

_____

_____

_____

Fulfilling and Satisfying Work

There is one and only you with unique talents and skills to offer this world. As you consider what is fun for you to do that is in accordance with your purpose, you will find success, fulfillment, and satisfaction in the way that you use your time and talents. We'll discuss the idea of your personal purpose, or your reason for doing what you do, in greater detail later in this book.

I believe that as you use your skills and talents in accordance with your purpose, work and life will be more enjoyable, satisfying, and valuable for you. The excitement that you feel for your work or the other ways in which you use your time will translate into a new level of excellence in your performance. That won't go unnoticed, and will most likely be considered more valuable to employers, organizations, and customers. When you do excellent work, you will be paid more.

A man who I will call Rob contacted me after reading my book, _The Path to Wealth_. He said that he had been using the daily practice and meeting with his CSO for over a month and got several intuitive leads to quit his job. He was relying on his CSO to give him leads about getting new work. Several months went by and Rob had not gotten any leads about a new job, so he asked for some help to create powerful goal statements. I asked him to describe his life after he had the perfect job. He shared that he would feel free, appreciated, and valued. He went on to say that he would have fun using his talents and would be rewarded with great benefits and higher pay than he had ever experienced before. As he focused on those goals with gratitude in his daily CSO meeting, and read stories about others who were working in their "dream jobs," he felt a lead two weeks later to attend an opening event for an arts organization. Attending this event seemed strange to him, but more than one person had mentioned the same event and he had a feeling that this was a lead from his CSO. At the event, Rob saw an old colleague who he had worked with 12 years prior. They had a pleasant conversation and upon hearing that Rob was looking for a job, the old colleague said that he knew a company president who was looking to hire someone with Rob's skills. The following week, Rob met with the president of a company that Rob admired. Five days after the meeting, Rob was offered a job that seemed to meet all of his goals, and which came with a larger salary and benefits package than he'd desired. As Rob became clear about his goal, he was able to notice leads from his CSO in order to experience it.

Please note, Rob didn't quit his previous job without being led to do so by his CSO. I advise that you wait to get leads from your CSO about the actions that you should take. Remember, if you don't understand the lead or feel unsure, ask for another lead. Then wait.

To begin to create your goal statements, answer the following questions:

What is your description of the perfect use of your skills and talents in work or other area of your life?

_____

_____

_____

_____

Describe what your life would be like as you use your skills in talents in wonderful work or other meaningful areas of your life. How do you feel? What are you doing? Who are you with? Where are you? How does achieving the goal affect others related to you, your company, your family, community, etc.?

_____

_____

_____

_____

Review your answers to the questions above and begin to create goal attainment statements which include the outcome of having your achieved your goal with gratitude.

> **Example:** "Thank you, CSO, that I now use my skills and talents in remarkable ways to work towards the success of my company, employer, coworkers, customers, suppliers, and my world. I am delighted that I am appreciated by my company and that I receive a minimum of $_____ of income per year for the great value and excellence that I bring to my job. Every day, I show up as the best person that I can be, and creative thoughts and actions flow through me to do the highest quality of work with ease. I feel increasing joy as I use my talents and skills in valuable and significant ways."

_____

_____

_____

_____

Harmonious Relationships

We live with an innumerable variety of species on one of billions of planets in a vast universe that has yet to be fully explored. In our day-to-day busy life, we somehow forget that and instead make ourselves the center of a universe in which everyone and everything is completely separate from us. When that happens, other people, animate and inanimate objects, and our situations can sometimes irritate us and feel like a burden. We can lash out, criticize, and even condemn others with our words, thoughts, and emotions. Instead of feeling better, most often we actually feel worse. There's a reason for that.

A relationship at its simplest is one being relating to another or relating to things. I believe that to relate is "to give an account of (create a story about) or to be connected to someone or something." In that connection, we have a valuable key: as we connect to and create a story about our relationship with others, their behavior, and their things, we are welcoming a similar account of us, our behavior, and our things into our lives. If our account or story is a positive one, we'll feel and experience positive things. If our account is a negative one, we'll have a negative experience instead. This is a law of giving and receiving. As we give out, we receive the same in return. This is actually good news!

If we want to have harmonious and positive relationships, we need to begin relating to and creating positive stories about others through our thoughts, words, and actions. To do that, I recommend that you create powerful goal attainment statements, use them daily in your morning practice, recite them throughout the day, and learn about others who have attained the kinds of harmonious and peaceful relationships that you'd like to achieve.

For example, a man named Tim had learned from his grandfather and father the phrase, "I'll be damned." He also learned to use condemning speech when someone did something that upset him (i.e., "Damn them!"). After attending one of my multi-week workshops, Tim discovered that his whole life was pretty "damned": his relationships at work were strained, his 15-year marriage had ended in bitterness, he was estranged from his brother and sister, and he had only a few friends—and even they were choosing to be less available to him over time. He described his relationships as a mess, and he wanted them to be more harmonious and fulfilling.

Tim made a decision to use the success system and partner with his CSO. He set the alarm and made it to his morning meeting every day. He created and recited powerful goal attainment statements, including: "I love everyone and everyone loves me. I forgive everyone and everyone forgives me. I am so grateful that I have wonderful and meaningful relationships and that I act as a great friend, partner, coworker, and member of my community. I feel appreciated and valued as I use my skills and talents to be helpful to others. I feel fully supported in return. I enjoy harmonious relationships with my family, friends, coworkers, neighbors, community, and my world. My life is good!"

Within a couple of weeks of using these statements in his morning meeting with his CSO and reading stories about people achieving harmonious relationships, he began to believe that it was possible for him to do the same. He didn't know how it would happen, but he believed it was possible. Tim worked to become more intentional about the words that he used to describe himself and others that he came into contact with, and to cease using the "damning" language.

A short time later, a coworker commented that she appreciated Tim's help on a project and asked some friendly questions. During the conversation, Tim was asked if he wanted to join other coworkers in a Habitat for Humanity project. Tim felt a strong sensation in his heart to say "yes." Over the course of a week, the team built a house for a family. Everyone had a wonderful time, and Tim felt appreciated and valued in the process.

I'm happy to report that Tim and his coworkers spend regular time together having fun, supporting the growth of their company, and doing meaningful projects to help others. Tim has also reached out to his siblings on a regular basis, and they are healing their relationships and getting to understand and appreciate each other more fully.

As you describe what you want the outcome of your goal to be with gratitude, and learn from other's examples that it's possible, you can shift your beliefs and notice more opportunities to achieve your goals.

To begin to create your goal statements, answer the following questions:

> What is your description of your perfect and harmonious relationships?

_____

_____

_____

_____

Describe what your life would be like as you relate to others in harmonious, satisfying, and happy ways. How do you feel? What are you doing? Who are you with? Where are you? How does achieving the goal affect others related to you, your company, your family, community, etc.?

_____

_____

_____

_____

Review your answers to the questions above and begin to create goal attainment statements that include the outcome of having your achieved goal with gratitude.

Example: "CSO, thank you that all of my relationships are valuable and harmonious. I appreciate everyone and everyone appreciates me. I enjoy supporting others and feeling supported and valued in my relationships. I find it easy and joyful to spend time with my friends, family, coworkers, and community having fun and sharing meaningful experiences. I am a great friend and have wonderful and harmonious relationships with others. I love my balanced life."

_____

_____

_____

_____

Recreation and Fun

What do you absolutely love to do? Where can you lose hours having fun? The answers to these questions could give you a clue to discovering your ideal recreation. I looked up the definition of recreation: "The refreshment of one's mind or body after work through activity that amuses or stimulates play; an activity that provides such refreshment."

What do you think of and how do you feel when you hear the words "refreshment," "play," "amuse," and "stimulate"? I can't help but smile, feel happy, and think of fun.

Recreation is a valuable tool to provide positive energy and balance. According to researchers who have studied successful aging, participating in activities that reduce stress provides tremendous health benefits. These benefits include better immune function, less illnesses and physical complaints, more energy, feeling more relaxed, sleeping better, better digestion, a calmer mood, more focus, and more positivity. Doesn't that sound like a perfect state to be in to notice more intuitive and subconscious messaging that will to help you achieve your goals?

I've found it interesting over the past 30 years speaking to people who are much older than I am and asking if there was anything in life that they would do differently. Most of the time, the answers are that they'd have more fun and not put so much pressure on themselves to be perfect. They wouldn't spend as much time at work, and they'd live a more balanced life so that they didn't neglect their family and friends.

In many corporations, employees are allowed to forgo using their vacation time because they get too busy. If you ever do this, consider making a change. It's important that you live a balanced life. When you do, I believe that you'll find that you'll be more productive and happy in all areas of your life. In my most recent healthcare companies, I asked my employees in January to schedule their vacation time throughout the rest of the year. I'm confident that planning for and requiring these recreation breaks helped them to relax, have fun, and come back to work rested and more productive.

Make recreation one of your goals and use the daily practice as part of your system for success to describe what you will experience as outcomes.

To begin to create your goal statements, answer the following questions:

What have you done in the past that was fun and refreshing?

_____

_____

_____

Describe that feeling and experience—not the "how" you got there, but the results of what you felt and experienced. Describe what your life would be like with regular experiences of recreation. How do you feel? What are you doing? Who are you with? Where are you? How does achieving the goal affect others related to you, your family, your workplace, community, etc.?

_____

_____

_____

_____

Review your answers to the questions above and begin to create goal attainment statements which include the outcome of having your achieved your goal with gratitude.

> **Example:** "I am so grateful that I have time for fun in my life and I easily schedule a minimum of ____ recreation breaks each year. Thank you, CSO, that I joyfully recharge my mind, body, and soul with fun activities with my family and friends and find that I am restored, balanced, and rested as a result. I return to work and normal activities more creatively charged as a result of having regular recreation in my life. I am fully supported with all of the money, time, and resources that I need to enjoy my recreation. I am incredibly productive in my work and other activities, more present and loving with my family and friends, and deeply connected to my spiritual source. Recreation supports my perfect health and I love my balanced and healthy life!"

_____

_____

_____

_____

Spiritual Connection

I believe there is an all-knowing power in our universe that is creative, intelligent, and abundant. We can connect to this power in fulfilling and meaningful ways to enhance our lives and achieve the life that we desire. Connecting to a spiritual source—God, Divine Intelligence, the CSO (or whatever name you give it that is comfortable for you)—is a common activity of successful people and entrepreneurs. As we deepen our connection to this spiritual power, we tend to feel more supported and confident in achieving our desires.

In the article, "Entrepreneurs Feel Closer to God Than the Rest of Us Do," published in the October 2013 issue of the *Harvard Business Review*, it was reported that Mitchell J. Neubert and three colleagues at Baylor University examined data from a survey that queried 1,714 US adults about their religious habits. Specifically, they investigated the connection between faith and the propensity to start a business. They found that entrepreneurs prayed more frequently than other people and were more likely to believe that God (Spirit, the CSO, etc.) was personally responsive to them. Dr. Neubert said, "Entrepreneurs seem to be more religious in a couple of small—but statistically significant—ways. They pray more—several times a week, on average—and are more likely to believe in an engaged, responsive God who takes a personal interest in them. You can see how the two might be related: If you think God cares about you, you're more likely to talk to him. . . . [T]hose findings might surprise people who assume that hard-driving businesspeople are too busy or greedy to make time for religion."

As you develop the belief that your CSO as your source of intuition can and will be available to you to guide you to achieve your desires, you will notice evidence of leads and opportunities that direct you along the path to your goals. Use your thoughts, words, and emotions to help shape your beliefs. Make time to meet each day with your CSO, the source of your intuition, to review your completed goals with gratitude. As you do so, you will notice that you will feel engaged with a spiritual partner who does take a personal interest in your success. Ideas and opportunities to accomplish your goals may surface more often as you use your daily success practice to achieve a valuable and deep connection to your source.

To begin to create your goal statements, answer the following questions:

> What is your idea of a deep, powerful, and meaningful spiritual connection?

_____

_____

_____

_____

Describe what your life would be like with a deep spiritual connection to the all-knowing power of the universe. How do you feel? What are you doing? Who are you with? Where are you? How does achieving the goal affect others related to you, your company, your family, community, etc.?

_____

_____

_____

_____

Review your answers to the questions above and begin to create goal attainment statements that include the outcome of having your achieved your goal with gratitude.

Example: "I am so grateful that I am in partnership with the all-knowing power of the universe as my CSO. I'm delighted that I am guided and directed to do that which is mine to do at all times, to experience my highest and greatest good as perfect love, peace, health, ease, joy, wisdom, abundant prosperity, and freedom. I'm grateful that I feel more connected to my source. Thank you, CSO, for this valuable and meaningful partnership that continues to grow in love and understanding each day."

_____

_____

_____

_____

Your World

In seasons of uncertainty, some people say that they feel helpless. It can seem that leaders of governments, businesses, and other organizations have all of the power to make decisions that we just have to live with. As we notice the problems of homelessness, unemployment, injustices, and more, we can get frustrated and fearful about the growing troubles. What should you do? Take action by doing the same thing that you do for your other goals: use your system for success to realize different outcomes that are consistent with what you desire. That can seem like a tall order, but trust me—you're more powerful than you think.

First, if you are upset and are experiencing negative emotions, you need to remove these so that you have room to receive your desired outcomes. To receive guidance from your CSO, you have to be in a calm state. Next, remember to be consistent in using your system for success. Each day show gratitude in a daily practice that describes the outcomes that you desire. This will help you notice evidence of your words made manifest. Remember the last time that you decided to buy a car and then you started to notice it on the road everywhere? Your subconscious filtered the hundreds of cars driving around and illuminated the ones that were consistent with your goal. As you focus more on the positive outcomes of your goal, your CSO can guide you along the path to see more evidence of what you desire in life manifesting.

If you describe a dismal future each day, you will notice more evidence of it. The same is true if you describe an abundant and hopeful future—you'll notice more possibilities to make that manifest. Successful motivational speaker and author Earl Nightingale described how powerful we are when he said, "Whatever we plant in our subconscious mind and nourish with repetition and emotion will one day become a reality." Your responsibility then is to choose what you plant—what you want to experience or what you don't want. Choose wisely.

For example, in my neighborhood we had a number of homeless people that were camping in tents under an overpass. Our neighborhood didn't have any facilities like water, food, bathrooms, or shelter to assist these people. Unfortunately, the homeless people chose to support their drug use and lifestyle by breaking into nearby homes and parked cars to obtain what they needed to live.

As you can imagine, the neighbors were quite upset after having their belongings stolen, and the police and other city and state agencies seemed to be unable to respond to the situation to prevent thefts from occurring in the future. Many of the neighbors were quite vocal in the online community and complained daily about the situation. Every day, I would wake up to see the neighborhood "news" posted about an increased number of break-ins and thefts. Over several months, it became like an addiction—I felt drawn to see what terrible news had happened overnight and even discussed the situation negatively with neighbors. While in the middle of this, I didn't realize that as I was expecting more of what I didn't want to happen, I was actually attracting more of it into our neighborhood.

One day during my daily success practice, my CSO reminded me through a strong thought that I have the power to choose what I focus my attention on so that it manifests in my life. That thought opened my eyes.

Every morning from that point on, I chose to be intentional and describe what I wanted the outcome to be. I used my daily CSO practice to describe a different experience. I created powerful goal statements like, "I'm so grateful that all people who live in and pass through my neighborhood are living happy, healthy, and safe lives with all of their needs met in lawful ways. All of us, our families, friends, neighbors, pets, and properties are divinely safe and protected at all times. We all treat each other with respect and live in our world together in peace, harmony, and safety." I then read this out loud daily with emotion to anchor it more fully within me, and imagined seeing myself in this "world" that I created with my words. I also stopped reading the neighborhood complaints online and spoke my goal for a peaceful and lawful neighborhood and world throughout the day to myself and with my neighbors.

Within two weeks, I got an intuitive idea from my CSO to bring all of the governmental agencies together at a community meeting to discuss the problem and possible solutions to protect the neighbors and serve the homeless in a meaningful way. I contacted the city council, the mayor's office, the police department, a state representative for our district, and the department of transportation (which owned the land that the homeless were using) to request that they all attend. They agreed to have their representatives there. I sent them questions and concerns from our community in advance so they could be prepared. I asked all community members to show up and behave in a respectful manner.

During the peaceful and orderly meeting with over 80 community members, many of the representatives discovered that their department policies actually prevented other government agencies from doing their jobs. As they got clear on the issues, they were able to make the changes necessary to serve everyone related to our neighborhood. The homeless were relocated to an area created by the city that had facilities that could assist them in a greater way. The neighbors felt safer. The city and state departments came up with solutions to work more cohesively together in the future. All related to this situation were benefited by it.

You have the power to choose to spend your time describing what your desired outcomes are in all areas of your life and in your world. Don't allow news stories and the opinions of others to become addictive and influence your expectations. Decide what you want as an outcome and, each day, repeat your desired goals and look for evidence that your CSO is guiding you through intuition and subconscious messaging to experience more of what you want. Take steps to follow the directions that you receive and enjoy realizing your goals in easier ways, because your CSO partner is doing its job in the partnership.

To begin to create your goal statements, answer the following questions:

What is your idea of living in a world that works for everyone?

_____

_____

_____

_____

Describe what your life would be like living in a world that works for everyone. How do you feel? What are you doing? Who are you with? Where are you? How does achieving the goal affect others related to you, your company, your family, community, etc.?

_____

_____

_____

_____

Review your answers to the questions above and begin to create goal attainment statements which include the outcome of having your achieved your goal with gratitude.

> **Example:** "Thank you, CSO, that I now live in a wonderful world that works for all and that I am free and happy. I'm grateful that all of us treat each other with respect and live together in lawful, peaceful, safe, and harmonious ways. I'm grateful that all of our needs are met and that we act as a community to support each other in greater understanding. Together we experience greater love, peace, health, joy, and abundant prosperity with grace and in perfect ways."

_____

_____

_____

_____

Whose Goal Are You Choosing?

Sometimes, influential people in positions of authority or who are respected in our families and communities have an idea for our success that isn't in line with what we would like to experience. It's important to recognize that your goals should have an element of joy and excitement. If you have a thought about doing something and it makes you happy, that may be because it's something that your inner self is causing you to notice—something that may be right for you, something that is in line with your purpose. I'll discuss how to discover your personal purpose in greater detail later in this book.

It's important that you choose goals that are fulfilling and satisfying to you. For me, I love to write. I like to write all of my business advertising and marketing copy. I like writing business letters and proposals. I enjoy writing newsletters. And I really enjoy helping people succeed and live prosperous and free lives through my writing and the sharing of my experiences. So, although I didn't have the strong belief that I could be a successful published author right away, I knew that I loved to write and help people succeed. That created the joy about my goal to become an author. Choose goals that you enjoy and make you feel happy, and you can use the system for success to achieve them.

If you decide to choose goals because someone else encourages you to, you may find that they are difficult to achieve. Most of us don't like to disappoint others, especially when they tell us how valuable we are. However, after agreeing to their idea of a goal that isn't in line with our own, we can sometimes feel unappreciated and experience some resentment. This isn't an uncommon cycle. It can repeat itself over and over again until you decide to break the pattern and realize that it is okay to say "no" to requests that aren't consistent with your goals and don't benefit you.

Ask yourself the following three questions before agreeing to someone else's goal for you. Let's look at how two women, Carla and Amy, used the three questions to figure out how to answer requests.

Am I required to do this, and will it benefit me and others related to the request?

It's important that you understand whether you're required to do something that is asked of you as part of your job or role in life. If you are not required, determine whether working towards someone else's goal has a value that is in line with your own goals so that you can feel good about sharing your time, talents, and treasures with others. If you're doing something for another person that isn't required, identify how you and others will benefit from your efforts. Will it make you happy and feel satisfied? If not, you may want to say "no" to the request.

Amy is a mother of three children, so when she's asked by her children to do what they want, she asks herself this first question to decide whether she's required as a mother to do what is asked of her. She may decide to say "no" to a request for a trip to the shopping mall with her daughter, but she wouldn't say "no" to transporting her to soccer practice because of the commitment that she and her daughter made to the team.

Carla is an amazing teacher and presenter, as well as being detail-oriented and organized. She works as a trainer in her company and loves to create classes and teach people how they can become fully engaged in their work. Often, she would get requests from her coworkers to perform other tasks because they said she was more detailed and organized than they were. Sometimes this was required as a way to support the harmonious action of the team, and Carla found that satisfying. In other instances, Carla would sometimes feel resentful and taken advantage of.

When requests aren't requirements, both women turned to the second question to make their decisions.

Am I the most skilled person to do the task and/or will I enjoy what I've been asked to do?

Because of a desire to please others, we can sometimes say "yes" to a request that isn't a requirement before determining if it's something that we'd like to do. If we spend our elective time doing things that we don't enjoy, it can deplete our energy and add more pressure to our lives in the form of stress. When we experience increased stress, it becomes difficult to notice intuitive leads from our CSO to achieve the goals that we desire. Perhaps it would be better to allow someone else who likes and enjoys those same tasks to do the project instead.

In Carla's world, getting requests that weren't part of her job and made her feel resentful would increase her stress because she also had to get her required work done with less time available to do it. She wasn't benefiting from agreeing to help. Due to the increased negative emotions that she had, she found it harder to recognize intuitive messages from her CSO to achieve her own goals. To recognize the messages from her CSO, she needed to be free from the negative emotions and in a calm and receptive mood. Clearly, she wasn't experiencing that. Before agreeing to any future requests to do something that wasn't required of her, Carla needed to ask herself this second question.

In an instance that was a turning point for her, Carla decided to let a requester know that she needed a week to think about the request for help. During this time, Carla decided that it wouldn't give her much joy to work on the project. But she wanted the requester to have the support he wanted, so she began to use her daily success practice to describe a completed goal where everyone received what they needed and felt fulfilled and appreciated at all times. She said, "Thank you, CSO, that all people who are right to work on this project successfully are easily available to do so, and we all are fulfilled, happy, appreciated, and satisfied in the process."

After using this goal statement as part of her daily success practice for several days, Carla had a strong intuitive thought to check in with someone else in the office who had been asking for additional work. When reviewing the project with the other employee and her supervisor, Carla learned that the employee wanted to do the project and would enjoy doing the work. This presented an optimal solution: to say "no" to something that Carla didn't want to do and clear the way to give the other employee the opportunity to do something she enjoyed. Everyone would benefit in this situation. Carla let her CSO guide her to take a step that was in accordance with her goal.

In Amy's case, it didn't take as long for her to realize that she wouldn't have much fun at the mall. She asked her daughter which of her friends she was expecting to meet there. After taking a moment to sit quietly away from her daughter, she felt inspired to pick up the phone to talk to the mother of one of her daughter's friends to ask about travel arrangements for the mall visit. Amy learned that the friend's mother had shopping to do and would be happy to pick up Amy's daughter and take her along.

Carla and Amy had only one more step to take: that of communicating the results to the original requesters. In other words, saying "no."

How can I stand in truth and integrity when saying "no"?

If you decide to say "no" to a request, put yourself in the requester's position. How would you like to receive the information if the roles were reversed? State your feelings and needs regarding the request and don't make the requester feel badly for asking for your help. Remember, there can be an outcome that works for everyone. As you focus on that along with your own goals and desires, your truth will be revealed in a compassionate way.

Carla asked to meet with the requester privately and conveyed that she didn't feel that she was the best person to do the special project. She then added that she had spoken to another employee with the skill set needed, and that this employee said that she would enjoy the work very much. The requester agreed that this was an excellent idea and thanked Carla for her help. She felt appreciated and happy operating in integrity.

As a result of saying "no" to the request, Carla was freed up to take on a different project that used her skills and talents in satisfying and enjoyable ways, and she enabled another employee to do the same. The company benefited from having two fully engaged employees doing valuable work that they liked. More people benefited from Carla's decision to say "no" to the request.

Amy let her daughter know that she understood that her daughter wanted to be with her friends at the mall. She also mentioned that after a long work week, she was tired and wanted to stay home to rest. Then, Amy offered a solution that allowed both herself and her daughter to receive what they wanted. She told her daughter that her friend's mother would be happy to drive Amy's daughter and her friend to the mall. They all had a great time, and Amy got a chance to be home to rest.

Focus on the outcomes of your desired goals. If someone decides that you should have a different goal, ask yourself the three questions above. Also, use your daily CSO practice to create a desired outcome that not only benefits you, but everyone else related to the situation as well. If you find in answering the questions that the request is something that you're required to do as part of your job or position in life, use your daily success system to describe greater ease, joy, and satisfaction in doing what's required. You'll find that doors and opportunities will open up to help you realize those outcomes while you complete the tasks.

A similar process can be used for other kinds of requests from family and friends. Operate in integrity and tell the truth, even if you believe that the requestor will be disappointed. It's important that you care for yourself and prevent resentment, stress, and other negative emotions from wearing down your physical body. Remember, when you experience negative emotions, you aren't as easily able to notice messages from your CSO that can guide you to take steps towards achieving other important goals.

Increased stress can have some long-term unhealthy effects as well. Writer Brian Krans summarized a variety of scientific studies in his article, "Nine Ways Stress Is More Dangerous Than You Think," published August 2016 in *Healthline*. Some of the dangers include difficulty in controlling emotions, increased risk of disease, adverse effects to your love life, deterioration of your teeth and gums, damage to your heart, increased weight gain, older appearance, weakened immune system, and long-term disability.

As you consider your requirements and what you enjoy before agreeing to a request for your time and talents, you will be in a better position to make decisions that enable you to experience better health, energy, and creativity in all that you do. More people will benefit from that!

The Daily Practice and Goals

All of my examples above are to be used as a guide to help you create your own powerful goal attainment statements. It's important that you use your own words that are consistent with your specific goals and values, and which have emotional meaning for you. Once you've created your powerful goal attainment statements for every area of your life, use the seven steps below on a daily basis to train your brain for success and stimulate your subconscious and spiritual intuition to guide you to take steps to achieve your goals:

Step 1: Read something inspirational

Step 2: Write a gratitude letter

Step 3: Speak with emotion

Step 4: Imagine experiencing your good

Step 5: Expect leads and follow directions

Step 6: Celebrate and note demonstrations

Step 7: End your day with forgiveness and gratitude

As you use gratitude and repetition in your daily success practice, you may begin to see evidence that your desires are being made manifest. You may also feel inspired to modify your words to be more specific in regard to your values and desires. Remember, your job is to describe your goals with gratitude as though they are completed. Your CSO creates the path and gives you one step at a time to take on the way to achieving your goals. You take the step, or ask for another lead. Eventually, you will take the steps to achieve your goals. I am celebrating your completed goals and success in advance with you now!

Section 3:

BELIEFS DRIVE YOUR BRAIN

Don't limit yourself. Many people limit
themselves to what they think they can do.
You can go as far as your mind lets you.
What you believe, remember, you can achieve.

— MARY KAY ASH

O ver the past 35+ years, I've recognized that as I achieved more of my goals, it became easier to follow the success system over time. I realized that success wasn't a secret or something reserved for only a few. Success is a system that anyone can learn to use. In addition to understanding the daily practice and partnership with your CSO, it's helpful to understand how your physical brain operates and can help you achieve more of what you want, more often.

Our beliefs and behaviors have been created over a lifetime. In that process, our brain remembers every time we had a goal in the past that we didn't achieve. It particularly recalls how disappointed we were. So, when we have a new goal that is different from what we believe is possible, our brain wants to protect us from disappointment. In doing so, it can prevent us from noticing possibilities to take steps towards achieving our goals. Our brain can seemingly put the CSO's intuitive messages on mute to try to protect us.

In her November 2010 article, "The Neuroscience of Changing Toxic Thinking Patterns," published on the Psych Central website, author and professional therapist Athena Staik, PhD, said, "If you do not have the life and relationships that you want, you likely do not have the thinking patterns you need to create the optimal emotional states, and thus actions, that would sustain your momentum in the overall direction of your aspirations. Unless you set an intention to make conscious changes, more often, change that occurs at subconscious levels tends to be self-perpetuating." In other words, if you don't change your beliefs to be in line with what you desire, you won't achieve your goals. Or, as author Louise Hay describes it, "If you accept a limiting belief, then it will become a truth for you." When your brain doesn't believe that it's possible for you to achieve a new goal, it won't be. You won't notice any leads from your CSO to take steps. Your use of the daily practice system for success is part of a conscious repetitive change process to guide you toward the successful life that you desire. This will assist you in altering your beliefs to be on par with the experiences and goals that you want.

Once you understand that your beliefs and behaviors can help or hinder you, you can incorporate that understanding into the system for success. You can use repetition to change your beliefs to be in line with what you desire. In doing so, you will create new and stronger beliefs that help you have the greater level of success that you want.

There is a scientific explanation for this. In our brains, each of us has a number of neural pathways that are associated with beliefs and behaviors that we have developed over a lifetime. These may include belief systems that you inherit from your family, your culture, friends, or coworkers—belief systems that are almost instinctive: "This is what I think. This is how I am. This is my personality. This is how it is." These neural pathways are major highways in our brains that have created major grooves, and it's very difficult to get away from them because they're so deeply imbedded. This may explain why you sometimes feel "stuck in a rut." You are stuck in a deeply grooved belief.

The good news is that you can strengthen a different neural pathway that is associated with the new belief and behavior that you want to experience. Think of repetition of your goals to change your beliefs this way: imagine walking through a field of tall grass as high as your hips. When you come back the second day, you may not see the path that you took. But, if you walk the same path, day after day, you'll start to notice it will create a sort of groove in the dirt at your feet. It will be much easier to move through the field.

This is what's happening in your brain. As you repeat the daily success system and make what you desire familiar and welcome, you're strengthening a "mind groove" as a neural pathway and creating a stronger belief that it's possible for you to achieve your desires. Once your belief shifts to one of possibility, your brain will take your CSO's messages off mute and you'll notice the intuitive directions to take the action steps that lead to your goals. This is a vital part of the system for success that is provable and repeatable if you're willing to use it consistently. You'll never be too old to live the life that you desire. Deepak Chopra shares, "The brain has a quality referred to as plasticity. The ability to form new neural pathways even into very old age. The brain is fluid, flexible, and incredibly adaptable to new experiences." As you make the choice to use gratitude with your daily success practice, you will be guided by your CSO to experience your new life!

When a goal is something that isn't normal for you, reading stories about and meeting people who have achieved that goal can help create your new beliefs faster. As Harold, the surfer/real estate agent, met other successful agents, he began to create new beliefs about being able to achieve his goals for success. As I met other authors and learned about their journeys, I started to believe that it was possible to become a published author. Once the belief starts to grow, you will notice more intuitive leads from the CSO to take steps along the path to your achieved goal.

For several months, I used the success system and daily CSO practice for my goal to become a published author. I met a large number of published authors and began to believe, "If they can do it, I can do it, too." Within a month of that shift in belief, I was led to invest in a company that puts writers together with talent like development editors, copy editors, illustrators, etc. I used myself and my book as a guinea pig and hired a developmental editor who helped me with structure.

Then, I got a lead to go to an event where I met other writers and heard about their experiences with rejection and struggles in becoming a published author. I decided that I didn't want the experience of struggle for myself, so I modified my goal statements to include an "easy and joyful" experience that I would have becoming a published author. This clarification process is something that you may do as well. As you follow leads from your CSO and take action steps, you may want to refine your goal statements to become more clear and consistent with your values and desires.

As I got clearer about my goals and strengthened my beliefs through repetition of the daily CSO practice, I started to run into more published authors, even at the grocery store. They seemed to be everywhere, which led me to feel more confident. My CSO was showing me that it was possible for me to become the published author that I wanted to be. My having a published book didn't seem impossible, and my brain took my CSO off of mute so that I could notice more intuitive directions. I did my part, which was to take action that was described through the intuitive leads or to ask for another lead. At that point, all that I had to do was to strengthen my beliefs and watch for and follow leads from my CSO.

This is what you need to do to—don't try to force anything to happen. Wait for the CSO to give you directions. American author and scholar, William Lyon Phelps said, "If you develop the absolute sense of certainty that powerful beliefs provide, then you can get yourself to accomplish virtually anything, including those things that other people are certain are impossible."

As you use your daily success system and make what you desire familiar and welcome in your life, you will grow in your sense of certainty that it's possible for you to achieve your desires in seeming miraculous ways. The impossible will seem possible for you. That's all that is required at this point in the change process: strengthen your beliefs through using your daily practice, making what you want familiar, and watching for leads from your CSO to take action steps.

The Fraud Factor

What happens when your goals are much bigger than anything that you've experienced, or when they are different than anything that you believe you can receive? Sometimes, you may want to abandon them. Don't do that! Use the daily success system and trust in your partnership with your CSO to direct you to successful outcomes.

As mentioned earlier, our strong beliefs and behaviors influence our decisions about possibilities for experiencing the good things that we desire. If we don't believe that achieving our goal is possible, we can feel fraudulent when we're repeating our goal statements in our daily practice routine for success. This is normal. I call it the "fraud factor." Let me give you an example.

My friend Marilyn is a very successful scientist. After taking one of my workshops, she mentioned that she wanted to be a paid singer—singing was one of her first loves, and she wanted to perform in a way that demonstrated appreciation for her talent and hard work. I asked her if she was any good at singing, and she sang for me. I got goosebumps; she sounded beautiful.

Each morning she wrote a description of her completed goal with gratitude, read it out loud, and imagined herself performing in front of audiences. She proclaimed each day in her CSO meeting, "Thank you CSO for the wonderful joy and success that I experience as I use my skills and talents to entertain others with my singing. I'm so grateful that I am paid well to sing part-time and enjoy myself immensely as I participate in events that benefit organizations that hire me and support their mission for serving their audiences in valuable ways. I love being able to sing and feel appreciated and satisfied in doing so."

After two months of using the daily practice, she told me that she was going to give up on her goal because she felt like a fraud. She hadn't received any leads or signs from her CSO that she was on the right track. I asked her some questions about her past as it related to singing.

She told me that at all family events and even in college with friends, she was always asked to sing. I learned that her parents had told her since she was a young girl that it was fine to sing as a hobby, but that it was foolish to work as a professional singer. They told her that professional singers never made any real money and that she needed a sensible degree and steady job to provide for her future. After hearing about these strong negative beliefs associated with singing for money, I asked her not to give up on her goal.

I explained that due to her old beliefs that began in childhood, her brain didn't believe that it was possible to be a paid singer and was putting the messages from her CSO on mute. I described the importance of changing her beliefs so they were on par with her new goal. I asked her to continue with her daily CSO meetings and to read stories about other singers who were paid to do what they loved. I asked her to get familiar with their stories and to meet other singers that were being paid to perform.

I'm glad to say she was willing to do all these things. As she learned about other singers' journeys, she realized that it was possible for her to have similar success. As she continued with the daily success practice and made her desires welcome, she was able to alter the beliefs to convince her brain that she was serious about achieving her goal. Once her brain stopped trying to protect her, she began to notice leads from her CSO though intuition and others that guided and directed her toward her goal of being a paid singer.

She felt intuitively guided to attend a fundraising event for the research center that employed her. During the event, a gentleman she didn't know walked up to her and introduced himself. As they chatted, he told her that he had been asked to organize an event at the local community center and that he had a budget for entertainment. Right then, her gut seemed to scream at her, "Tell him you're a singer!" Marilyn immediately did so. When she mentioned that she was a singer, she was asked to audition the following week. Soon, she had her first paying gig! She met her goal through an unusual occurrence—a seeming miracle—and a man who walked up to her at an event.

This type of occurrence can happen for you, too. Today, Marilyn is still a successful scientist and loves her work. But, she now has part-time paid work that allows her to use her singing talents in wonderful and satisfying ways. She achieved what she desired and is very happy.

The way that we create a stronger belief in line with our desired goals is to use repetition and gratitude in our daily success practice and to make what we want familiar and welcome. We make something familiar by learning more about it, by learning about the journeys of others who have achieved what we want, or by experiencing it ourselves.

If you want to do something new, get familiar with other people who are doing what you want to do. Learn more about their stories and their journeys to achieve their goals. If you want to experience something different, see if you can try it out. If it is a new car, test drive one. If it's a new home, go to open houses for similar homes and imagine what it would be like to live there. If it's a new relationship, read stories about and speak to others who have developed similar kinds of successful relationships. If it's improved health, find people who have achieved the kind of well-being that you desire and learn what they did to realize their optimal health. Mahatma Gandhi explained the power of beliefs this way, "Man often becomes what he believes himself to be. If I keep on saying to myself that I cannot do a certain thing, it is possible that I may end by really becoming incapable of doing it. On the contrary, if I shall have the belief that I can do it, I shall surely acquire the capacity to do it, even if I may not have it at the beginning." Whatever we choose to repeat to ourselves strengthens our beliefs.

Just like Marilyn—the scientist who wanted to be a singer—you can choose to use the daily success system to overcome fraudulent feelings. Meet daily with your CSO and review your goals in order to strengthen new beliefs and make what you want familiar and welcome. As you become familiar with the desired good that you want, it will be easier for you to imagine having it. When you believe that it's possible to experience your desired outcomes, your spiritual intuition and your subconscious will show up more often in obvious ways to point the way for you to achieve it.

Don't Try to Make Things Happen

In the process of changing and strengthening new beliefs, it's important to wait for leads from your CSO. Don't try to make things happen while you're waiting for a lead. Because we can get impatient from living in a society that likes instant gratification, we may want to take some action that our rational mind recommends. According to Florence Scovel Shinn, "Man's dreary desires are answered drearily, and his impatient desires, long delayed or violently fulfilled." She goes on to tell the story of a woman who was constantly losing or breaking her eyeglasses. In Shinn's conversation with the woman, they discovered that the woman often said in vexation, "I wish I could get rid of my glasses." Her "impatient desire" was being "violently fulfilled." What she should have described with gratitude was her life with perfect eyesight so that there would be no need for glasses at all.

When you try to force something, your rational mind considers only the actions that it deems as possible. As you listen to and take the action that your rational mind recommends, you may limit the possibilities that your CSO can illuminate for you. Let me give you an example.

I know a woman who wanted to help her brother with his business. While considering options to take action, she had a number of thoughts about steps that she could take, but she still felt a little uneasy. However, instead of waiting to get a confirming lead from her CSO, she was swayed by her brother's wants and chose to make a $60,000 investment in an opportunity that, when he explained it, made rational sense.

Shortly after that, things started to go wrong. Instead of describing what she wanted and requesting additional leads, she worked toward the rational idea that she, her brother, and their partner had committed to. More things went wrong.

Finally, in exhaustion and frustration, she surrendered. She began to be intentional in using her daily success system to describe what she wanted: "CSO, thank you for the fulfilling and satisfying use of my skills and talents in profitable ways. I'm so grateful that my brother, our partner, and all related to the venture that we've started are guided and directed by you to do our part to live happy, healthy, and prosperous lives. If this business is the right one for us, open doors and point us along a clear path. If not, slam the door shut and direct us elsewhere to realize our higher and greater good."

About that time, the woman's brother had an opportunity to spend more time with his wife and grandkids in another state, which would bring him greater joy. He started spending less time on the business. The partner experienced an emergency that required him to care for a family member who needed his help. He also started spending less time on the business. As the woman continued to meet with her CSO daily, she had a strong thought to contact a friend. After contacting this friend, she was offered a position working in another industry altogether.

As the woman, her brother, and their partner stopped trying to force something to happen, doors were opened for the right manifestation of their goals to unfold. They dissolved the business, and now, several years later, they are each enjoying their lives and using their talents in more joyful and prosperous ways. Unfortunately, the woman lost the $60,000 invested in the failed business. However, within a year at her new position, she was given a raise and stock options that were valued at more than $63,000. There was no loss in the all-knowing universe, and the money spent was restored to her.

Your CSO partner, as the source of intuition, can assist you in achieving any goal that you desire. It's important that your system for success includes patience to wait for leads from your CSO. When you get a lead, don't allow your rational mind (or someone else's) to talk you out of taking a step. If you're unsure if some direction is from your CSO, simply ask for another lead. Then wait for it: don't try to force an action.

In one of my previous businesses, I used my daily success practice to describe a completed goal with gratitude of $400,000 in revenues to be received by my company by a particular date. Each day I stated powerful goal statements; "CSO, thank you for the minimum of $400,000 that our company receives by the end of next quarter. I'm so grateful that our company is now able to serve a greater number of customers in valuable and meaningful ways. All related to our company are blessed and happy with the products, services, and successful outcomes that we enable under grace and in perfect ways."

During my next trip to visit a current customer in another city, I had dropped off my bags at the hotel and hopped back into the car to go to a grocery store that was five minutes away. I then had a strong thought about a grocery store that was fifteen minutes away. That didn't make sense, and my rational mind told me so. It said, "May, it's 9:00 p.m. It's much too late to be driving across town to a grocery store when you know that there is a perfectly good one nearby that has everything that you need. And, your meeting tomorrow is at 8:00 a.m., which is 5:00 a.m. in the time zone you came from. You will be too tired if you don't get a good night sleep. Just go to the closest grocery store."

Can you identify with how your rational mind would say that to you? It will always try to reason through every situation and suggest that you abandon what it considers to be foolish thoughts. This is the time when you should either take the step and drive across town to the other grocery store, or figuratively stomp your foot and say, "CSO, if that message was from you, give me another lead." Then wait for your spiritual intuition to chime in if it needs to. I asked for another lead.

As I waited in my car for a few minutes, I had another strong thought about the grocery store across town. I also had some intuitive ideas that seemed to say, "May, it's true that it's 9:00 p.m. here, but it's only 6:00 p.m. at home. It's too early for you to go to sleep anyway. And, who knows? Maybe everything that you want will be on sale at that grocery store. Just make the drive." So, I did.

As I walked into the grocery store, a man that I recognized was walking out. He was someone I had met six months earlier who worked for a very large potential customer and I hadn't been able to schedule a meeting with him prior to my trip. We both stopped to say hello. As we were finishing with our visit, he said that I could come to make a presentation to his company while I was in town. That presentation led to several more meetings, and eventually my company received a contract worth over $400,000 in the time frame that I had been requesting in my daily CSO meetings.

Your rational mind wouldn't have imagined that this could happen. Many of us have been taught through our families, schools, and jobs that we should create a goal and determine every small step to take on the way to achieving it. While that can work, it's been my experience that even though steps provided by the CSO don't always make rational sense, they can produce even greater results. As we follow leads from our CSO, the steps that we take can assist us in achieving goals in easier ways that are extraordinary or unusual. Seeming miracles can become typical occurrences more often.

Sometimes while waiting for a confirming lead from your CSO, your rational mind will get impatient and still want you to take action. It may think of other things that you could do in order to convince you that it knows best. If you try to make something happen or force action as a result of following only your rational mind, you may delay your goal from manifesting in an easy and joyful way. You may find that it becomes a struggle and it's difficult to achieve what you want. That's because you're trying to do it yourself. Your CSO partner will simply wait for you to finish. If you're not successful in achieving the outcome that you tried to force to happen, your brain will recognize disappointment and go back into a protective mode. It will put your CSO partner's intuitive messages back on mute. You'll have to start all over building your beliefs in possibility to convince your brain to take the CSO off mute.

Don't try to make something happen. Don't force action. Your CSO partner can be relied on. Develop some patience to enable your goals to manifest with greater ease and joy. Wait until you get a lead and follow the intuitive directions from your CSO. Let your CSO partner do its job in the partnership and commit to doing your job.

Your primary job when creating new beliefs is to strengthen them. Use the daily success practice and make what you want familiar and welcome. In the example I used about becoming a published author, what was important was to continue strengthening my beliefs with gratitude and repetition. I continued to wait for leads from my CSO. I wasn't to try to make anything happen, even though I thought of lots of rational ways to get a book self-published. That could have set me up to try something that wasn't in line with my goal to be a published author. If that happened and it didn't work, my brain would return to a protective mode and prevent me from noticing intuitive leads, signs, and messages from my CSO.

As I continued to use the daily success system to strengthen my beliefs and make what I wanted familiar, I began to notice more intuitive leads from my CSO that directed me to take action. A noticeable lead that I got was to contact a woman who came to mind. I didn't know why or for what goal, I just knew that I had to contact her. When I did, she asked me to become a small-group facilitator in a class that she was teaching. I agreed. In the class, I met another facilitator, who I'll call Aaron. He had just self-published his own book and showed me a copy. His profession was in an industry that was completely different from the topic of his book. That helped me to gain even more confidence, and strengthened my beliefs—if Aaron could do it, so could I.

At that point, I truly believed that I could get my book published and become an author. I knew that the CSO would guide me to the right opportunity. I didn't know how that was going to happen, so I kept using my daily success practice and asked my CSO for more leads. Two weeks later, out of the blue, Aaron sent me an email about a workshop that was going to be put on by the president of a publishing house. I signed up and went.

At the workshop, I felt completely out of my league. There were Hollywood producers, MDs, PhDs, radio show hosts, and many published authors. I felt nervous about being there. My rational mind offered that it was foolish for me to be there since I was not as skilled as the others in the room. I felt like a fraud and wanted to leave. But, I reminded myself that I had been led there by my CSO. Instead of succumbing to my fearful feelings, I kept saying to myself, "CSO, I know that you guided me to be here, and I'm grateful for that. Show me what I'm to learn. Thank you for giving me more definite leads." I stayed and completed the workshop, which I found very helpful for restructuring what I had already written to date as my manuscript. Along the way, the hosts of the workshop found out about my book as well.

The day after the workshop, I was contacted by the publishing house to learn more about me and my book. Before the end of the call, I was asked to submit my unfinished manuscript. I sent it two weeks later. A month later, the publisher decided to publish my book.

When you receive a lead from your CSO, either take a step or ask for another lead. As you are taking steps, show courage and repeat your gratitude statements for achieving your desired goals. Continue to request that the CSO guide you with more leads. If you are on the right path, doors will open up. If not, the CSO will slam doors shut and point you in a new direction.

American mythologist, author, and lecturer Joseph Campbell explained his view on a key point to any success system: "Follow your bliss. If you do follow your bliss, you put yourself on a kind of track that has been there all the while waiting for you . . . [Y]ou begin to meet people who are in the field of your bliss, and they open the doors to you." He continued, "If you follow your bliss, doors will open for you that wouldn't have opened for anyone else." I agree. Doors will open for you as you are guided by your CSO to take steps that are in line with your blissful desires.

To illustrate this, let me tell you about Stacy, who had a very strong relationship with her family. Helping them gave her great joy. After learning that her elderly aunt in a distant city would appreciate having Stacy closer, she made a decision to move to be near her and some other relatives. Stacy's relatives praised her decision and said that their aunt would be grateful to see her more often.

As she prepared for her trip, Stacy said, "CSO, thank you for guiding and directing me to live the divine plan for my life in which I experience my higher and greater Good at all times. If this move is the right one for me, make it easy and joyful. If not, slam the door shut and point me in a new direction."

Within a few days, things regarding her relocation started to go wrong. Stacy couldn't find a way out of her rental lease agreement and would have to pay to leave her apartment early. Friends told her that her planned move wasn't the right thing for her to do, since she'd be leaving a great job that allowed her to advance quickly in her career. Her car even broke down unexpectedly, so she wouldn't be able to pack up and drive to the new location. As Stacy continued to use her daily success practice and showed gratitude for her fulfilling, happy, and prosperous life, she had a strong idea to go to a yoga class. That was unusual because she had never been to the yoga studio that came to mind. But, she felt that the lead was from her CSO and went anyway.

At the yoga class, she met a woman who invited her to coffee. During the friendly conversation, the woman mentioned that two years prior she had moved because relatives wanted her to, and it was a disaster. She described how after she arrived, the other relatives expected her to be a primary caregiver. She felt taken advantage of and she experienced stress and anxiety because she wasn't trained to be a healthcare provider. She wasn't even being paid to help her relative. She began to resent her other relatives who weren't helping at all, and it caused a strain in their relationships. She went on to say that she decided at the end of a year to move back to the city she lived in now. She got a great paying job and visits her relatives on occasion to help out. She also sends some money each month to help pay for her relative's care from qualified providers.

After hearing this woman's story, Stacy felt that this was a message from her CSO. She thanked her CSO and asked for more leads. The next day, she got a strong idea to speak with her aunt's physician. With permission from her aunt, Stacy learned that the care that her aunt needed required full-time attention.

Stacy thanked her CSO for the information and decided not to move. She got together on the phone with other relatives so that they could come up with a different plan to help her aunt with qualified caregivers. They each decided to contribute some money toward the care of their aunt, and everyone seemed happier about the outcome. Within a few months, Stacy did advance in her career and received a promotion with an increase in pay to more than cover the amount that she committed for her aunt's care. She also received more paid vacation time so that she could visit her aunt more often. Stacy achieved her goal for a fulfilling, happy, and prosperous life while doing something she loved—helping her relatives.

Be sure to use your daily success practice to describe your completed goals with gratitude. Then, wait for leads from your CSO, who will guide you to the life you desire. When you get a lead, show courage, take a step, and continue to request more confirming leads. If you try to force a situation to make something happen, you may experience what you don't want to happen or delay the manifestation of your desires. As you stay focused on your completed goals with gratitude, doors will open and you'll be led on a path that is extraordinary and unusual. You will see that miraculous experiences are becoming typical occurrences for you.

Doubts and Fears Delay Miracles

As we move away from old beliefs that don't serve us, there is something within us that can try to pull us back into experiencing our former behaviors—our former self-imposed limits of good. This includes all of the limitations that we don't want to experience anymore, such as lack, unworthiness, ideas about less than optimal health and finances, etc. We remember how we coped with those old situations, and, although we didn't like what we were experiencing, we knew how to operate. Author Betsy McKee Henry described it perfectly when she said, "Emotions like anger, worry, and disappointment are habits, and like other bad habits, can be broken." We developed a habit of handling and surviving in that old life. To achieve something better, we need to break an old habit and make a change.

The reason there can be a pull to take us back to a familiar place is fear of the unknown future that we desire. When that pull is strong, our view of the future can be distorted. We may think situations are going wrong, when in fact they are going right. These are the times when we have to show discipline and courage to move through fears and doubts to the new life that we want to experience. The inventor Thomas Edison said, "Many of life's failures are people who did not realize how close they were to success when they gave up." Don't give up on what you desire for your life. Use the daily system for success and keep moving through the fearful thoughts—don't choose to camp there.

As you begin to shift your beliefs to be in line with what you desire, understand that it's normal for doubts and fears to try to sabotage your efforts and return you to a place where you know how to cope. Your old self loves you and wants to keep you safe; the new place where you achieve your desired goals is unknown and uncertain. It can seem like a threat to your old self.

Alex grew up as what he called "the runt" of his family. He was smaller than most of the other boys in class and got bullied throughout school. He got into a habit of expecting to be treated poorly— that was his experience throughout his life. As an adult, he learned to stay quiet and become invisible at his job while doing what was expected of him.

After taking one of my workshops, Alex decided that he wanted to experience a new level of success and happiness. He described each day in his daily success practice: "CSO, I am so grateful that I now live a powerful, fulfilling, healthy, and prosperous life. I feel happy, strong, and capable of doing my work with excellence, and I have valuable and meaningful relationships at work and in my personal life. I treat everyone that I come into contact with in a respectful way, and I feel appreciated and respected in return. I love who I am, and I love my free life." After using goal attainment statements like these for several weeks, Alex started to feel different: he felt more powerful. These feelings allowed him to speak up at meetings with creative ideas and to go out of his way to be helpful to customers and coworkers.

Unfortunately, at first many things at work seemed to go wrong. Alex perceived that his bosses and coworkers were upset with him for changing. Whether this was true or not didn't matter. To Alex, they appeared to blame him for problems that came up. Managers in his company told Alex that there wasn't any room to grow and advance in his career, so he'd have to settle for the position that he was in.

Alex began to have doubts and fears about his value and future. He was not feeling appreciated and respected at all. His old thoughts rose up to advise him that he should settle for the job that he had and go back to being the ordinary and invisible person that he used to be. He even started to miss what he remembered as the easier and calmer life of his past. These thoughts and feelings were trying to pull Alex back to his old life where he knew how to cope and operate.

When Alex described this situation to me, I asked him to show courage and use his words, thoughts, and emotions to prime his brain for success all day long. I assured him that the internal thoughts, feelings, and perceptions that he had about what was going on at work were lies that his old self was projecting to pull him back to his old life. I assured him that if he used his daily system for success along with additional affirmations all day long, he would be successful in changing his beliefs and quieting the "old self" thoughts. He would then be able to attract what he desired as he followed leads that his CSO provided.

Throughout the day, Alex repeated dozens of times, "I'm so grateful that I live my powerful and fulfilling life! I am happy, healthy, wealthy, and free. I am fully supported with a minimum of $_____

to take care of my living, giving, and entertainment expenses, and I feel valued and respected at all times as I value and respect others."

During one of his commutes home on the bus several weeks later, Alex saw a sign for a business that seemed to sparkle in the light. He hadn't noticed this sign before and thought that it was interesting. He continued with his daily success practice, and things at work seemed to be getting worse. More people seemed angry with him, and he couldn't explain it. He didn't like going to work anymore. He felt defeated and alone. I told him that something big was just around the corner and to continue with his daily success practice. I asked him to continue to repeat his success statements anytime he had doubts and fears. He agreed and did this.

Two weeks later, on another commute home, the bus that he was riding had an accident. All of the passengers had to get off and wait for another bus to arrive. Alex started to walk in the direction of his apartment. As he passed the sign that he had seen sparkle previously, he felt an urge to walk into the business. He was greeted by a friendly receptionist who told him what the business did. During the discussion, a man who worked there came out to speak with the receptionist and met Alex. As they talked about the business and the man learned what Alex did for a living, he asked Alex if he'd be interested in applying for a position with their company.

I'm happy to report that within a month, Alex accepted a position working for that new company. He loves his job. He feels powerful as a creative contributor to the success of his company. And, as a bonus, he and his coworkers spend time outside of work together. He's developed friendships and is able to volunteer for organizations that he is passionate about. Alex feels valued, respected, and appreciated, and he has a career path before him that allows for promotions and powerful participation for the success of the company. When everything appeared to be going wrong at his old company, everything was really going right.

All of the old doubts and fears that Alex had about his self-worth and value rose to the surface so he could put them out of his life forever. He used the most powerful tools—his words, thoughts, and emotions—to achieve the life that he desired. You can use these powerful tools, too.

As you focus your attention on your desired new life and talk about it, think about it, and feel emotionally about it, you magnetize yourself to experiencing it. Whether you do this for things that you want or things that you don't want, you will notice evidence of the areas in which you focus your attention manifesting.

As mentioned earlier in this book, you may have proved this when you last bought a car. The words, thoughts, and emotions of your focus on the car you wanted helped you notice the model driving around everywhere, in the midst of thousands of cars on the road. The same thing will happen when you use your words, thoughts, and emotions deliberately and intentionally to focus on your desired goals and outcomes.

Alex continued to use his words, thoughts, and emotions to drown out his doubts and fears and to proclaim the powerful life that he desired. He saw the signs that his CSO gave to him about the new business that he now works for, which was a step to achieving his goals.

Each time you get fearful about a new desire or goal manifesting, any time that you feel filled with doubt as to whether or not it is possible, recite out loud your new truth in the situation. Use your words to describe your completed goals with gratitude. It's impossible for you to think of something fearful or doubtful and speak something contrary out loud. Try it right now. Think of something negative, but speak something positive out loud. Your spoken word will take the lead and overpower any thoughts and feelings that you have.

You may have to speak your goal and truth statements hundreds of times to quiet the doubts and fears. As you do this repeatedly each day, those fears and doubts will show up less and less over time. This is a vital part of changing your beliefs. Scholar and philosopher Thomas Aquinas said, "We can't have full knowledge all at once. We must start by believing; then afterwards we may be led on to master the evidence for ourselves." As you use your words, thoughts, and emotions to change your beliefs, you will be in a state that allows your CSO to lead you to see the evidence of your realized goals.

Create some powerful goal statements in advance and keep those with you at all times to use if you are ever doubtful or fearful. To help you with this, answer the following questions:

> What doubt or fear do I have about achieving my goal? (For example, Alex had the doubt that he wasn't valuable and powerful enough to succeed and live a successful and prosperous life.)

_____

_____

_____

If nothing was in the way and I could achieve what I desire, how could I describe it as completed with gratitude? (For example, Alex described his goal for a powerful, healthy, happy life that was prosperous and filled with mutual respect and value for himself and others.)

_____

_____

Write down your description of your completed goals with gratitude, and keep copies with you at all times. Whenever you feel fearful or filled with doubt, recite these statements over and over until the fear and doubt subside. You may have to repeat them dozens of times the first day, but each subsequent day you will have to say them less and less. Eventually, your brain will believe that you're serious about living your realized goals, and the fearful thoughts will stop. That's when you will begin to notice more opportunities from your CSO to take steps to achieve what you desire. Don't give up. Show disciplined courage to describe what you want and to quiet your mind. This will allow you to notice the intuitive directions from your CSO to achieve your desires.

Power in Agreement

Alex found it helpful to speak with me about his desired outcomes and the fears and doubts that showed up. This is a powerful point. I believe that others who are not emotionally attached to your situation and who support you in achieving your goals can be powerful allies in helping you manifest what you desire in life.

I like to use the analogy of being at the top of a mountain. The mountain signifies a challenge or old belief. When you're at the top, you can't see what the entire mountain looks like; you see only one small part of it. As you receive support from others, you're able to get down and move away from the mountain so you can see the entire mountain from a distance. With support from others, you will recognize what the truth is in the situation. As you find strength in their descriptions of the truth that are consistent with your desired outcomes, you'll be able to see that your perceptions, fears, and doubts were lies trying to pull you back to your old familiar and limited life.

I encourage you to surround yourself with people who support you in realizing your goals for the new life that you desire. Choose your supportive allies wisely, and make sure that they sincerely want you to achieve your desires.

In 2007, I formed a group with five other women who wanted to achieve more of their goals. We continue to meet once a month for two hours and enjoy a potluck and friendship. During the meeting of our group, which we call a "Blessed Women Sangha," we each share what we've experienced during the previous month and what we'd like to experience during the following month. As we describe what we want, we use the system for success format and describe our goals as though they are already complete with gratitude. Each member of the Blessed Women Sangha feels supported and appreciated. Each has a voice and the opportunity to ask for advice and compassion for any situation that they are experiencing. Our new goal statements are written down and distributed to each member at the end of our Sangha. Over the following month between meetings, we all commit to recite out loud each of the completed goal statements for the members of the Sangha on a daily basis.

We define a Sangha as "an association, assembly, company or community." It's a name that is often used as part of the Buddhist teaching to refer to a community of monks or nuns—those who practice spirituality. Other people refer to their groups as prayer groups, power or accountability groups, friend groups, and even support groups. Regardless of what you call your group, there is power in all of you being in agreement and focused on the same achieved goals and outcomes.

As I recite each of the goal statements for our Sangha members each day, I add power to their manifestation. I see each of us living the outcome of our goal statements and feel joyful that they are being completed. Sometimes I have an intuitive idea to share with another member of my group. Sometimes they have an idea to share with me. Many religious traditions say that there is tremendous power in agreement for a particular outcome.

In the Christian tradition, Jesus is often quoted as saying, "If two of you shall agree on earth as touching anything that they shall ask, it shall be done for them of my Father who is in heaven." Whether you believe the literal meaning of Jesus's message is not the point. I believe that these words are meant to show us that there is power in agreement. When others support us by knowing our goals as manifest, the goals will likely be achieved. Metaphysical traditions teach that a collective consciousness is power that can shift outcomes. People can lean into the confidence and strength of others to manifest the completed outcomes of their desires.

It's easier to know perfect health, happiness, prosperity, and success for another person when you are not emotionally attached to the outcomes. This kind of confidence and power of our words, thoughts, and emotions can be used to help others feel supported, and they can do the same for us.

Misty Copeland, one of America's top ballet dancers, said, "Be strong, be fearless, be beautiful. And believe that anything is possible when you have the right people there to support you." Find a group of people to support you and whom you can support. Make a choice to meet on a regular basis and share your desires as well as your challenges. As you help them with your words, thoughts, and emotions to achieve their ideas for success, you will find that they are helping you do the same.

Science has shown that when we focus on something in partnership or as a group, we exhibit more power and tend to make better decisions. In a 2010 report called *Optimally Interacting Minds*, research led by Bahador Bahrami (of the Interacting Mind Project at University College London and Aarhus University in Denmark) was designed to determine whether two participants made better decisions about visual images while working together, or while working in isolation. The participants were instructed to pick the image that contained a target. They each initially decided on an answer alone. Then, if the duo gave different answers, they had to discuss the possible answers and create a joint decision. To test whether two heads really are better than one, these collective decisions were then compared to performance when each person worked alone. The results showed that two heads were indeed better than one. The volunteers were able to combine weak neuronal activities residing in two separate brains to maximize performance.

When we focus on a successful outcome for someone else, we enable spiritual intuition to flow through both of us for their benefit. Be sure to share your goals and desires with people who support your idea for success, and remain open to your CSO's guidance to come through them or other channels for your benefit.

I've included my Sangha meeting ground rules and agenda format in the Appendix if you'd like to form one of your own. Choose people who truly support you and who you want the highest and best good for to take part in your Sangha.

As a reminder, in your Sangha or in your daily success system, you need to stay focused on what you want, not what you don't want. Our words are powerful tools that help us to receive whatever we describe and focus on. Unfortunately, we often give voice to what we don't want instead of what we do want, and then we're surprised and disappointed with the results. Be clear with your group that you should all describe each of your desired outcomes, not what you don't desire.

Using your words, thoughts, and emotions to describe your completed and realized goals in advance with gratitude will enable your subconscious and your spiritual partner's intuitive leads to show up more often and in more obvious ways to help you all.

Section 4:

PURPOSE TO PROSPERITY

The two most important days in life are the day you born and the day you discover the reason why.

— MARK TWAIN

As you are thinking about what you want in all areas of your life, some consideration should be given to discovering your personal purpose. Purpose is commonly defined as: "the reason why something is done or used; the aim or intention of something; the feeling of being determined to do or achieve something; the aim or goal of a person; what a person is trying to do, become, etc." Put simply, I believe that my purpose is why I exist.

For me, discovering my purpose enabled me to create more powerful goals in every area of my life. Achieving them became more satisfying, fulfilling, and prosperous. This will be your experience, too, once you discover and live in accordance with your purpose.

Focus on answering the question, "Why am I here to do what I do?" The answer to this will help you to discover your personal purpose.

If you're a business owner or executive, you should also determine the purpose for your company and convey this to all of your employees, customers, suppliers, and other stakeholders. As an employee, find out what the purpose of your company is so that you can be in alignment with the mission and values in a more meaningful way.

Believing in your personal purpose and the purpose for your company/employer will keep you motivated to work towards the goals and outcomes desired. Purpose is the fuel for passion and accomplishment.

Purpose Fuels Your Success

Now that you have tools to incorporate a successful system for achieving greater goals with more happiness and freedom, it is helpful to discover the motivation for sticking with a goal. As we discussed earlier, sometimes we can give up on goals that don't feel right for us. We may not notice any intuitive leads from our CSO to guide and direct us on a path to achieve those goals. This could have to do with the beliefs and behaviors that are associated with neural pathways in our brain. But, it could also be due to our goal not being in alignment with our purpose.

To fuel your drive to achieve the success that you desire, you should be clear about your purpose. Your purpose is the "why" you are here to do what you do. As you look at your life and what you love to do, you'll begin to notice elements of your purpose.

As a child, I discovered that my purpose was to bless others and be blessed. Every large goal that I've accomplished in my life has had an element of this purpose. As I grew in my understanding about my life, my work, and how I related to other people, I created variations of this purpose. For example, I have a specific purpose for writing books and traveling the world to teach the success principles described in my books. My purpose now is to elevate prosperity and freedom for all. Can you see that this purpose is still consistent with the purpose I had as a younger person—to bless others and be blessed?

All successful people have demonstrated their understanding of their purpose. Bill Gates started at the age of 13 to use computers and spent most of his free time creating software programs, which he started to sell at 15. He believed a long time ago that everyone should have easy access to a computer at all times. Oprah Winfrey described her purpose when she said, "I've known since I was a barefooted young girl playing school on the Mississippi dirt road that ran adjacent to my grandmother's front yard that I had an inkling for storytelling and teaching." As a young girl, Oprah used to gather her friends together and "play school," and she served as the teacher. She commented later that she knew that she was going to be a teacher, but didn't recognize that it would be through the media. As you discover what you've been passionate about throughout your life, you can get some clues about your purpose.

According to a 2014 study published in *Psychological Science*, a journal of the Association for Psychological Science, researchers discovered that knowing and living in accordance with your purpose can help improve your life at any age. "The research has clear implications for promoting positive aging and adult development," says lead researcher Patrick Hill of Carleton University in Canada. He added, "Our findings point to the fact that finding a direction for life and setting overarching goals for what you want to achieve can help you actually live longer, regardless of when you find your purpose. So, the earlier someone comes to a direction for life, the earlier these protective effects may be able to occur." Knowing your purpose and setting overarching goals as part of your daily practice for success can help you live a longer life.

One of my favorite authors, Wayne Dyer, described how he experienced increased success once he got clear about his purpose: "When I chased after money, I never had enough. When I got my life on purpose and focused on giving of myself and everything that arrived into my life, then I was prosperous." As he discovered that his purpose involved giving, he did things that allowed him to give more. He felt happier and prospered more as a result.

You can live in alignment with your purpose. In doing so, you will find greater satisfaction in achieving goals that are related to your purpose. Once you are clear about your personal purpose, you'll find that you have increased energy and vitality to fuel your drive on the journey to achieve your right goals for success.

To begin the discovery process for your purpose, I'd like you to answer a few questions. I've listed them below along with some space for you to note your answers.

Describe a few things that you've done repeatedly since you were a child which gives you great joy. What activities would you do that were fun and where you lost several hours being engaged?

_____

_____

_____

_____

For example, I know a man named Steve who lived in a small town as a child. He told me that as early as ten years old, he loved to take apart electronics and put them back together. He could spend hours joyfully figuring out how telephones, toasters, and other small appliances operated. As he grew a little older, he rode his bike to the appliance store and spoke with the repair people about his understanding. He read books and service manuals from manufacturers. He loved to learn how the electronic appliances worked and how to fix them. He also liked to help in other ways and learned from service people that were hired to do repairs at his family home. He watched the plumbers, carpenters, and other contractors do their jobs and asked lots of questions to learn more about what they were doing. As he learned more about the repairs, he was able to fix some of the future problems that came up on his own and received praise from his parents and siblings in return.

As you remember what you loved to do as a child, see if any of those things are still fun for you. When I was a child, I loved to write stories and turn them into plays. I asked many of my friends in the neighborhood to perform the different parts. We would spend hours, day after day, practicing until we felt satisfied that our play was terrific and ready to perform. I designed the set and decorations with my friends. We hung sheets as our stage curtains in a carport. I had my friends bring chairs from their homes to line up in the driveway for the audience to sit on during the performance. We invited the families on our street to attend to see our production for 25 cents each and were sold out each time. We even sold bags of popcorn and lemonade as refreshments. We had such a great time. As soon as one play was performed successfully, I'd start planning for the next one.

What I learned about myself as I began to discover my purpose is that I love to tell stories that are easily understood and entertaining. I also learned that I like to make money through a fair exchange of value, like the money that was exchanged for seeing a performance of our play and the refreshments that we offered. Steve learned that he liked to use his intelligence to solve problems and receive praise from his family.

After you answer question #1 above, write down what you are learning about your childhood self in the section below.

_____

_____

_____

Describe a few things that others have told you that you are good at doing. Ask others what they think you are good at, if you don't already know. What have you done that others have said you've done well, and what talents and skills did you use that were enjoyable to you?

_____

_____

_____

_____

For example, Hanna is often referred to as an exceptional encourager and champion for others to achieve their goals. Hanna's coworkers, family, and friends told her that they love to talk to her about their problems and successes. They noticed that as Hanna listened to them, she tended to ask clarifying questions and was very present and undistracted in hearing their answers. Through this process, people said that they felt empowered and encouraged to take action and were supported without judgement by Hanna. They also remarked that often, they would come up with powerful solutions on their own simply by speaking with Hanna and answering the questions that she asked. They always walked away from conversations with Hanna feeling like she was their cheerleader and that she wanted them to succeed in all areas of their lives.

As you discover what others tell you that you're great at doing, see if any of those kinds of things resonate with you and are fun for you to do.

After reviewing what people told Hanna she was good at doing, she realized a few things about what she liked to do. She enjoyed connecting with people. She liked to listen and ask people questions so that they could discover some truths about their situations. She liked to guide them to generate ideas about how those truths can serve them to achieve a greater sense of freedom and success. She liked to receive success in return.

After you answer question #2 above, write down what you are learning about the common traits that others say you are good at expressing and what you like to do.

_____

_____

_____

_____

List a few skills and talents that you feel successful in using. What talents do you enjoy using today? How do you like to spend your free time?

_____

_____

_____

For example, Steve noted that he loved to use his intelligence and problem-solving skills to help others, and he enjoyed receiving gratitude and appreciation in return. Hanna said that she liked being approachable and a great listener who helped people find the truth in any situation. She also enjoyed receiving gratitude and appreciation, as well as satisfaction and fulfillment in return. For me, I enjoy telling stories to benefit others in their personal and professional lives. I love to help others to succeed. I like to succeed as well.

After you answer questions in #3 above, write down what you are learning about what you love to do and experience.

_____

_____

_____

_____

Now that you've completed this exercise, think about the phrases, talents, skills, traits, and characteristics that have shown up in all three areas: childhood, feedback from others, and what you feel that you're good at doing now. The descriptions that are common to all three areas might give you some ideas about your purpose—the "why" that you're here and what you love to do. Begin to write those words and phrases down, and see if you can put them into one to two sentences that are a complete description that feels right for you.

_____

_____

_____

_____

Steve came up with: "I use my intelligence and ability to make other's lives easier and less complicated. I live abundantly and free." After discovering his purpose, Steve made a goal to live his purpose and to achieve goals for financial freedom. He used the daily success system with gratitude and consistency to describe his completed goals. Within a year of using the daily practice and following the leads from his CSO, Steve was led to start his own company. Several years later, Steve can truthfully say that he lives his purpose. He operates his own successful plumbing company with 20 employees.

Hanna described her purpose as, "I am a cheerleader who empowers and supports others to find truth, freedom, and abundance. I am blessed with support, freedom and abundance." As Hanna became clear about her purpose, she created powerful goal attainment statements to use in her daily success practice. She described her completed goals with gratitude and followed leads that she got from her spiritual partner to take steps to achieve the life that she desired. Over the next several years, Hanna enjoyed seeming miraculous events manifesting in her life that provided her with more time, opportunities, and funding to become a minister and real estate investor. As a minister, she helps people discover their truths and receives financial support to do so. She was also directed to an employment position that allowed her to earn equity as part of her employee package, while working for a real estate investment group that she supports and helps to become successful. In return, she receives a paycheck and stock in the company. She feels that she has more freedom and abundance in her life.

For me, my overall purpose as the "why" that I'm here is to use my skills and talents in satisfying and fulfilling ways to bless others and be blessed. That purpose continues to be the right one for me. However, I have gotten a little more specific when describing certain goals, like writing this book and teaching these principles: I share valuable skills, talents, and information that help to elevate prosperity and freedom for all. I am blessed with prosperity and freedom.

Discovering your purpose can provide the necessary fuel and motivation that you need to be successful. You'll find that when you're creating goals for your desired life, your words and ideas will shift into alignment with your purpose. Successful author and speaker Jack Canfield said, "If you can tune into your purpose and really align with it, setting goals so that your vision is an expression of that purpose, then life flows much more easily." Achieving the life that you desire will become easier if you align your goals with your purpose.

As you shift to the belief that it's possible for you to achieve your goals, you will notice more intuitive leads from your CSO to take steps along your path to fulfillment. Extremely outstanding and unusual events will happen more frequently with less of the work. Miracles will turn into typical, normal occurrences.

Purpose Energizes Your Company

Now that you've worked to discover your personal purpose and can use that to fuel your passion to achieve more of your goals, you can do the same for your company. If you own your own company, you should create a purpose statement and let all related to your company know what it is. If you are an employee for a company, learn the purpose for the company or help to create its purpose statement.

If employees, customers, suppliers, and other stakeholders see how a company's purpose can lead to success, they will use that to fuel their support for the company. Most successful companies have a purpose, a "why" they exist to do what they do. This is different from "what" they do in their day-to-day business.

Dutch company ING says that their purpose is "empowering people to stay a step ahead in life and business." That's very different than what they do, which is providing financial services. Digital advertising company REA Group says that their purpose is "to make the property [real estate] process simple, efficient, and stress-free for people buying and selling a property." The description of "what" they do is to operate Australia's leading residential, commercial, and share property websites.

The Kellogg Company describes their purpose as "nourishing families so they can flourish and thrive." Do you see how this is so much more than "what" they do, which is to manufacture and sell food products? If you were an employee, supplier, customer, or investor, wouldn't you feel good about "nourishing families so they can flourish and thrive"? You want to create a purpose for your company that explains "why" your company exists to do what they do, which will motivate all stakeholders to support its purpose.

To do so, think about what each of your stakeholders would say about why the company you work for exists and the benefits that they see and receive as a result of your company operating. You might even want to ask yourself and some of the stakeholders with whom you have great relationships these questions. Write down your thoughts below:

You:

_____

_____

_____

Employees:

_____

_____

_____

Customers:

_____

_____

_____

Suppliers:

_____

_____

_____

Investors:

_____

_____

_____

Board Members:

_____

_____

_____

Community:

_____

_____

_____

For example, as a child, my friend Moni loved to create art and products using what she found in nature to help others be happy. She used flowers, leaves, sticks, sand, rocks, and other natural things that she gathered as part of her creations. She discovered that her very simple purpose was "to help people to enjoy the wonderful gifts of nature and feel happy."

As a young adult, Moni worked as a massage therapist and began to create essential oils out of natural ingredients to use in her practice to help her clients. She studied the healing elements of different plants to create her oils so that she could help her clients reduce inflammation, be more relaxed, enjoy detoxification, and loosen up tight muscles as part of her massage therapy. Her clients raved about their experiences, and she was always fully booked for six to eight weeks in advance.

Other therapists learned about what Moni was doing and asked that she create products for them. She did that and earned quite a bit of money as a side business. This new business grew to the point that she stopped being a massage therapist and focused on the growth of the natural product business. As she learned more, she grew her product offering to include natural essential oils, lotions, and bath salts, which she sold not only to other therapists, but also to retail stores across the country.

After taking my workshop called "Purpose to Profits," Moni realized that she needed to define the purpose for her company. She was already clear about "what" her company did: "We create and distribute high-quality aromatherapy products designed to help support people on their path of healing body, mind, and spirit." But, she needed to have a purpose statement that described "why" her company existed. After considering what her personal purpose was and what every stakeholder would say about why her company existed, she came up with her company purpose statement: "To promote health and well-being through sharing the pure powers of nature." Can you see how her company purpose is different and so much bigger than what the company does? Imagine how satisfied her employees feel in knowing that their company exists to promote health and well-being for all.

If you own your own company, create a purpose statement: the reason "why" your company exists to do what it does. If you work for a company, ask to see its purpose statement. This is not the same as a mission or vision statement. If your employer doesn't have one, try to create one for them so that you can feel more motivated to do the best job that you can in order to support the purpose and growth of the company.

In my last company, our purpose was "to save lives." That's it—that's why we existed. This was very different than what we did which was "to create and distribute software, equipment, and workflow systems to automate the drug distribution process in health systems so that they could be more productive, save money, and improve patient safety." As we did our jobs well, we helped hospitals improve patient safety and save lives. I hope that these examples clarify that the purpose of a company is much bigger than what the company does. It's the reason why a company exists. Your company/employer has a unique purpose, too. Because of it, you may find that you're more motivated to do your job and become increasingly successful in your efforts.

In 2015, Ernst and Young sponsored the creation of a Harvard

Business Review Analytics Services report titled *The Business Case for Purpose*. Researchers determined that companies with a purpose beyond profit alone tend to make more money. The global survey of 474 executives found, "In those organizations where purpose had become a driver of strategy and decision making, executives reported a greater ability to deliver revenue growth and drive successful innovation and ongoing transformation."

They went on to declare as "a new leading edge" . . . "Those companies able to harness the power of purpose to drive performance and profitability enjoy a distinct competitive advantage." As your company becomes clear about its purpose and engages all stakeholders to work toward the bigger idea, successful outcomes of growth, satisfaction, and excellence will be more likely to happen. Everyone related to your company will benefit.

Creating a purpose for your company and letting others know about it is important to generating passion within your company. Please understand that you can't just state your purpose—you've got to demonstrate it in the actions your company takes. I recently read a *Fast Company* article called, "How Entrepreneurs Can Harness the Science of Intuition to Make Smarter Decisions" (April 2017). The article relates how Jeff Sinelli, CEO of Which Wich, was standing in line to meet one of his heroes, Container Store CEO Kip Tindle, at a conference. When it was his turn, Sinelli pressed his business card into Tindle's hand. Something was printed on the back of the card. Tindle read it out loud. "Some people want to make superior sandwiches. Some people want to make the world a better place. We want to do both." Tindle looked up and asked Sinelli, "So Jeff, what are you doing to make the world better?" Sinelli didn't have an answer because the statement was a tagline. He thought about an answer and said, "When I get back to Dallas, I'm going to make peanut butter and jelly sandwiches and give them out to the community." This year, Which Wich will give away its one-millionth free sandwich. The program has helped the company to demonstrate their purpose. This has enabled Sinelli to stay energized through rapid growth and keeps employees engaged in the repetitive work of making fast-food sandwiches. The company has become more successful as employees are energized with a sense of purpose.

Follow the steps above to review your personal and company purpose at least once a year. As you grow in your understanding of yourself and the world in which you live, you will find that your purpose becomes more clearly defined. This is a wonderful part of our human experience. I hope that you find that living your life with purpose provides you with greater satisfaction, fulfillment, joy, and prosperity.

Going from Big to Bigger

Since success is a system, you can continue to use it for larger and larger goals. You can use the same system-for-success process to achieve even more.

For example, Elizabeth had been using her daily system for success to achieve a number of goals. She was convinced that any goal was possible for her to manifest as part of her partnership with her CSO. So, she decided that she would start to work on her largest and biggest goal: repairing her relationships with her siblings. There had been a falling out years prior when her father died and the children couldn't agree on the division of the inheritance. There were lawsuits and hurtful behavior, and she and her siblings hadn't spoken in years.

As Elizabeth used her daily system for success to describe harmonious relationships as her desired outcome, she felt called to send loving cards, emails, texts, and invitations to her siblings over the next few years. She didn't receive any responses, but she continued to make the effort while proclaiming that her relationships were repaired and harmonious. She felt more at peace as she read stories and spoke to others who had successfully healed very difficult relationships in their families. She remained hopeful and continued to follow leads from her CSO to take action.

Several years later, Elizabeth's uncle died and all of her siblings were at the funeral. During the reception, their aunt asked all of the siblings to get together in a private room. The aunt reminded her nieces and nephews that life was too short to fight and that it broke their uncle's heart to know that his nieces and nephews were estranged. She asked them to figure out a way to repair their relationships before it was too late.

Through the rest of the reception, Elizabeth faced her fear and went up to each of her siblings to say how sorry she was for what had happened in their past and offered to do whatever they felt it would take to repair their relationship. She was received warmly and that was the start of achieving her biggest goal yet—having harmonious and loving relationships with her siblings. She knows it will take more time to bring her goal to completion, but she's confident that she's being guided along the right path by her CSO.

Bigger goals might take a little longer for you to achieve simply because of your strong beliefs and emotional ties to the situation. That's okay. Keep up with the daily system for success, and you will find that your CSO will guide you to recognize opportunities to take action.

I hope that you feel some confidence in knowing that success is not a secret, it's a system. Anyone can achieve the success that they desire if they understand how to use gratitude along with the daily practice system to partner with their CSO as the source of intuition, intelligence, and power. This is an infinitely abundant universe, and your CSO can guide you in seemingly miraculous ways to achieve all that you desire, require, and more, with less work on your part. You can experience a life where manifesting miracles becomes a typical occurrence for you.

Summary

I'm delighted that you've chosen to live the miraculous life that you desire. Your choice to incorporate a provable and repeatable system for success will produce more of what you want to experience. Following the daily success practice and partnering with the CSO—the source of intuition—opens up the intelligence of the universe to you. No longer will you be limited to what your rational mind believes is possible. All things are now possible as your CSO guides you to take steps along a path that it creates to fulfill your dreams and desires. A new sense of freedom and joy will be yours as you use the daily success system with gratitude.

To experience more apparent miracles as part of your typical experience in life, continue to use the daily system for success.

Following is a summary of the system:

Morning practice to meet with your CSO: Describe your completed goals with gratitude.

Daytime practice to interact with your CSO, expect and recognize leads and steps to take, and celebrate and note demonstrations with joy and gratitude.

Evening practice to release and make room for the good things that you desire.

Create and use powerful goal statements with gratitude to attract your desires.

Choose goals that are right for you, not goals that others have for you.

Recognize that it's your brain's love for you—the part that tries to protect you—that puts your CSO on mute. Demonstrate consistency while loving it back and unleash your CSO's voice.

Be patient when waiting for leads. Don't try to force something to happen.

Be disciplined in using your success system even when there is a pull back to an old way of life.

Discover your purpose to add fuel and passion to your goals and success.

After you achieve a goal, create a bigger one and use the same system for success.

It is my great joy to share with you this simple system for success to help you achieve all that you desire. As you use the daily success practice, partner with your CSO to guide you, and create powerful goals that are right for you and in alignment with your purpose, you will find that you experience greater joy, satisfaction, prosperity, and peace with less of the work.

You will see that unusual events as miraculous experiences become typical for you; you will begin to see opportunities to help others to learn what you know. You'll notice more occasions when you can share your success stories. Taking the time to share will help someone else experience the success that you have become familiar with and which you have welcomed into your life, so don't hold back. This is an abundant universe. As you give of yourself to others, you will be blessed and receive even more in return. Thank you for sharing this universe with me.

Appendix

INSPIRED READING

*Nothing in life is to be feared, it is only to
be understood. Now is the time to understand
more, so that we may fear less.*

— MARIE CURIE

I am delighted that you have made the commitment to partner with your CSO as the source of intuition to help you achieve your goals. I know that you will experience more of the good things that you want as you develop your relationship with your new partner. To help you get started right away with your daily practice, I've included a list of suggested readings, a sample of one of my gratitude letters used in the morning practice, an outline to form your own support group or Sangha, and a list of affirmations that you can refer to as needed. All of this is designed to support you in your growth and understanding of spiritual and practical principles so that you can experience the life that you desire.

Books that are suitable for the reading portion of the practice are listed below, but feel free to use any books of your choice that put you into a receptive mood for understanding that the universal power is operating through us all.

The Game of Life and How to Play It, Florence Scovel Shinn, 1925

Your Word Is Your Wand, Florence Scovel Shinn, 1928

The Secret Door to Success, Florence Scovel Shinn, 1940

This Thing Called You, Ernest Holmes, 1948

The Dynamic Laws of Prosperity, Catherine Ponder, 1962

The Dynamic Laws of Healing, Catherine Ponder, 1972

As a Man Thinketh, James Allan, 1902

Think and Grow Rich, Napoleon Hill, 1937

The Seven Spiritual Laws of Success, Deepak Chopra, 1994

The Way of the Wizard, Deepak Chopra, 1997

The Four Agreements, Don Miguel Ruiz, 1997

The Power of Your Subconscious Mind, Joseph Murphy, 1963

The Power of Now, Eckhart Tolle, 1997

The Power of Intention, Dr. Wayne Dyer, 2005

Sample CSO Letter

Following is a sample of one of my gratitude letters:

Dear CSO,

Thank you for all that you are and all that you do to guide and direct me to live the divine plan for my life and experience my highest and best good in all ways at all times.

Thank you, CSO, that I experience perfect love. I love everyone, and everyone loves me. I love myself and am loved. I bless everyone, and everyone blesses me. I bless myself and am blessed. I forgive everyone, and everyone forgives me. I forgive myself and am forgiven.

Thank you, CSO, that I experience perfect peace and am poised, confident, comfortable, and connected to you at all times.

Thank you, CSO, that I experience perfect health with a physically fit, trim, and toned body that is strong and healthy, eternally youthful, and increasingly more beautiful, energized, and filled with vitality.

Thank you, CSO, that I experience ease and joy in all that I do. I live a charmed and wonderful life where everything makes way for the good life that I desire. I'm grateful that I easily and joyfully use my skills and talents in satisfying, prosperous, and fun ways to bless others and be blessed.

Thank you that I am a successful best-selling author with more than _____ books sold and that all readers and others related to my books are happy and blessed by them. I'm so grateful that I am a highly sought after and very well-paid speaker, teacher, and presenter. People with large audiences hire me for more than _____ events each year without delay under grace and in perfect ways.

Thank you, CSO, that I share valuable information with all audiences and others related to these events so that they can experience happier and more prosperous lives.

Thank you, CSO, that I experience perfect wisdom and freedom.

Thank you that I am prosperous with more than

$\_\_\_\_\_$, which is now mine by divine right to use and enjoy, bless others with, and invest and increase, all as you direct. I'm so grateful that I am debt free, cash-flow positive, and profitable at all times in all ways.

Thank you, CSO, that all peoples who live in and pass through my neighborhood and world are living healthy and safe lives with all of their needs met in peaceful and lawful ways. All of us, our pets, and our properties are divinely safe. We all treat each other with respect and live together in our world in harmony and peace.

Thank you, CSO, for my husband Don. We are so blessed and happy at all times.

Thank you for Indy the cat, my family, friends, neighbors, coworkers, customers, students, audiences, suppliers, vendors, and every bit of creation in our world.

For all of this good and more, I give great thanks. I am grateful and recognize that you are the infinite power and intelligence in the universe that guides me. I now release these words to the universe and it is done. And so it is!

Love you,

May

Sangha Ground Rules

Following are the ground rules and agenda format for my Blessed Women Sangha group.

Confidentiality: What is said in the group must stay in the group. It is inappropriate to discuss what is said in the group with anyone outside the group. However, it is permissible to share your own experience of the group. Share only your own experiences, never the experiences of another.

Sharing: An open and authentic atmosphere is provided to encourage members to share their truth at the level that is appropriate for them. There is no need for any group member to share anything that they would choose not to reveal. The group connection will deepen when members share their experience and the results instead of each detail of the process to arrive there. Members are there to share their experiences and demonstrations and can choose not to share at all if they don't want to. All are to be honored for being the intelligence and power of Spirit.

Listening: Allow others to share their feelings and experiences freely. Do not comment, give advice, or detract from another's sharing. Do not tell a similar story on their time. This is commonly called "cross talk" and should never occur at small group meetings. People will find their own truth through being able to share openly and hear their own thoughts spoken. They don't want advice; they want a witness. Each person has their own distinct journey of learning and discovery. Learn to lovingly listen to let others learn. As we honor this process, people will feel safe and will, thus, open up in deeper ways, discovering more and more about themselves. No "fixing."

Respect: Group members can show respect for one another by not interrupting or having side conversations. Attempt not to leave the room during the meeting, but if you must, exit quietly in the time between one sharer finishing and another beginning. This will show respect for the person currently speaking.

Focus: Group members agree that they will stay focused and on the subject to ensure that the meeting flows smoothly and each member has time to share. In addition, all members should recognize that we're here to develop a deeper understanding of Spirit, not to create an argument to fight and win.

Challenges: Small groups are not designed as therapy. If someone feels the need for further help, find a professional for assistance or ask group members for a referral to an appropriate resource.

Time: The opening and closing times for each gathering should be respected. Members need to agree to be on time and present when the meeting opens. It is the groups' responsibility to keep track of the time to ensure that the group meeting ends at the agreed upon time.

Sangha Meeting Outline

Opening

Open with prayer. Use the following (or create your own). You may choose to have one member read the opening, or read it together.

> "Together we open this time, recognizing each other as an expression of Spirit. During this sacred Sangha, we move past all appearances and affirm the truth and wisdom for each person here. We know that each of our endeavors thrives and prospers as each of us thrives and prospers in perfect fulfillment. In blessed oneness, we support each other in prayer, knowing only good for all. And so it is!"

Checking In

Each person shares her insights, revelations and experiences since the previous sangha. Questions to answer:

> "What was your prayer request last time?"

> "Have you noticed any demonstrations as a result of this prayer request?"

"What do you see as the next step to achieving your goals?"

"Did you experience challenges/fears in this process that may feel like blocks?"

Prayer Requests

Share goal or prayer requests, one for each team member. Word them as already complete with gratitude.

Close

Close with prayer. Use the one below, or create your own. Choose a volunteer to read the closing, or read it together.

"As we close this Sangha, we again acknowledge the universe to be all there is. We turn our attention to the nature of Spirit that we choose to acknowledge today and gratefully accept the expression of that nature in our endeavors. We know that whatever Spirit is, we are. As Spirit is intelligence, so are we. As Spirit is love and freedom, so are we. So, in faith and expectation of the all-knowing power of the universe showing up in its perfection in our lives, we claim . . . " [Each person adds their prayer request here as you go around the circle.]

"In sweet gratitude, we affirm the good that has been claimed by each person here. With absolute faith, we gratefully acknowledge the immediate unfolding of this good. We release these words to the perfect activity of the universe and know that our good is manifesting right here and right now and that day by day we witness the blossoming of Spirit's magnificence. It's all good— and so it is!"

Adjourn

Reconfirm the next three meetings date/time/place.

Sample Goal Statements

Following are some powerful goal statements that can inspire you to create your own for your morning practice or that you can use throughout the day to stay focused on what you desire.

To Realize Perfect Health and Well-Being

"I am grateful to be physically fit, healthy, and happy at all times in all ways."

"Thank you that I am growing increasingly more beautiful and healthy every day in every way."

"As the perfect creation of the universe, my perfect health manifests. Thank you, CSO, for guiding me to my good health."

"I am smarter, happier, healthier, and wealthier each and every moment of each and every day."

"Every cell in my body is filled with healing light."

"I'm so grateful that I now move through life in a perfectly healthy and happy body with increased energy and vitality. I feel free!"

To Realize Improved Wealth and Finances

"Thank you, CSO, for guiding and directing me to receive more than $_____ into my life each month in interesting ways. I am now financially free."

"All that I require and more is easily and joyfully available to me. I am grateful to use and enjoy a minimum of $_____ each year. I now help and support others and invest and increase the amount with grace and in perfect ways."

"I'm so grateful that there are no limits in this abundant universe. As I believe, I receive. I now receive more than $_____ this year, and I am free and happy."

"I delight in how easy it is for me and my family to enjoy financial freedom with overflowing amounts of resources that support all of our living, giving, and entertainment expenses. Life is fun with the CSO as my supply partner."

"I now follow directions and leads from my CSO to do what I'm to do. I am grateful that I now live a financially free life where I am cash-flow positive and profitable at all times in all ways."

"I'm so grateful that I now thrive and prosper with overflowing amounts of money and resources to easily and joyfully afford my life. I'm now debt free, cash-flow positive and profitable at all times."

To Realize Fulfilling and Satisfying Work

"Thank you, CSO, that I now use my skills and talents in remarkable and satisfying ways and I am prospered, happy, and fulfilled at all times."

"I'm so grateful that I am a valuable member of my company and feel appreciated and valued at all times. I value and appreciate all in my company and am rewarded financially with a minimum of $_____ each year to use and enjoy with grace."

"I am grateful to experience intuitive insights to be of great value to my company, customers, coworkers, and all stakeholders related to our company. I am consistently rewarded and appreciated for the work that I do."

"Thank you, CSO, for guiding and directing me at all times in all ways to use my skills and talents to work towards the success of my company, coworkers, customers, suppliers, and all stakeholders related to our business. I am successful in return."

"I am grateful to work in a position that is vital to the company purpose, and I bless all stakeholders as we prosper and grow to do higher and greater good in our world."

To Experience Harmonious Relationships

"I cast all burdens of poor relationships on the CSO within. I'm grateful that we all are free to be loving, harmonious, and detached from the tyranny of fear."

"Just as everything in universal power is harmonious and perfect, everything in my relationships is harmonious and perfect. Thank you that all are happy."

"Everyone and every situation is a strong and valuable link in the chain of good for me and my life. I'm grateful and value everyone."

"Adverse people and situations are a part of my good. Thank you, CSO, for working through all people to bring my good to pass."

"I love everyone, and everyone loves me. I bless everyone, and everyone blesses me. I forgive everyone, and everyone forgives me. I am grateful that I am loved, blessed, and forgiven. We are all free."

"Thank you that I now have harmonious and wonderful relationships with all of my family, friends, and everyone related to my company/workplace. We all respect and value each other, and I feel respected and valued at all times in all ways."

To Experience Recreation and Fun

"I'm so grateful that I now live a balanced and wonderful life where everything makes way for me and my good. I have the time and resources to experience a fun, satisfying, and rewarding life."

"Thank you, CSO, that I enjoy regular recreation that rejuvenates me. I am well rested and easily recognize your leads that direct me to my highest and best good always."

"I'm delighted to be present with my family as we vacation together a minimum of ___ times per year. We experience deep and loving connections and enjoy our wonderful life of freedom."

"I'm so grateful that I have the support from my company to enjoy regular recreation and fun. I easily and joyfully receive the time, money, and resources necessary to enjoy my vacations and return to work well rested, more creative, and more productive. I and my company benefit from my balanced life."

"Thank you, CSO, that I am free to live my balanced and wonderful life with regular recreation and fun activities. I, my family, friends, and all related to my company benefit immensely from this peace and balance in my life."

To Recognize Spiritual Connection

"I am grateful that I recognize and have the courage to follow leads from my spiritual partner to direct me in all of my affairs. My life is good!"

"Thank you, CSO, for revealing yourself to me in obvious ways. Give me definite leads. Show me what is mine to do under grace and in perfect ways."

"Thank you, CSO, that the divine plan for my life unfolds perfectly."

"Only what is true of the CSO is true of me. I am inspired and led to make right decisions quickly in every situation."

"I am grateful that the CSO guides and directs me to experience my highest and best good at all times."

"Thank you, CSO, for going before me to make my way clear."

"I'm so grateful that all that is for the highest and best good for me now manifests without delay, with grace and in perfect ways."

To Realize a World That Works for All

"Thank you that I see evidence of a peaceful and harmonious world where all of us treat each other with respect and dignity."

"Thank you, CSO, for showing me what is mine to do as part of the safe and loving world that I live in."

"I am grateful that all people in my world are living safe, healthy, and happy lives with all of their needs met in lawful ways. We are all divinely loved and prosper."

"Thank you, CSO, that I and all of my neighbors, family, pets, and properties live in safety and harmony with all that we require easily available from the bank of the universe."

"I'm so grateful that all in our world express love toward themselves and each other and we work toward our mutual success with excellence and kindness."

"We are so blessed with increase and plenty as we bless with success others in our world."

"We are all magnetic to our good and live together in peace and harmony."

To Increase Success

"Thank you, CSO, for going before me. My success is assured."

"I'm grateful to use my remarkable skills and talents in satisfying and fulfilling ways and am rewarded with more than $____ per year that flows easily and joyfully into my life."

"I enjoy my work and feel appreciated by my company, my coworkers, my suppliers, and all related to my work in any way. I am grateful to be valued and happy."

"All our customers are happy, satisfied, and delighted with our products and services. They tell all their peers at other companies to buy from us, too. And they do."

"I'm grateful that my business takes off with a huge increase in sales. All related to this are blessed by it."

"Thank you, CSO, for guiding me to never-ending supply. I accept and receive the huge success that is mine now."

"I'm grateful that the CSO now guides and directs me in all of my affairs and my work. I am valued, appreciated, and financially rewarded with more than $_____ in income as my company experiences increased sales and profits. All related to my company are happy."

To Overcome Fear

"I cast this burden of fear on the CSO within, and I go free to be loving, happy, and harmonious, detached from the tyranny of fear."

"What universal power has done for others, the CSO now does for me and more."

"I am grateful to be guided and directed by the CSO's divine love and wisdom. I make right decisions quickly."

"There is nothing to fear, for the CSO makes my way clear and easy. I'm grateful that there is nothing that can hurt."

"Thank you, CSO, that only that which is for my highest and best good manifests in my life."

"I deny that my past history has anything to do with my future success. I am so grateful that I now go forward to experience perfect satisfaction, joy, health, and prosperity. I am free!"

To Erase or Neutralize Mistakes

"I bless the past and forget it. I bless the future, knowing it is filled with wonderful opportunities and success. I live fully in the present now and am blessed with all I desire or require and more."

"I'm grateful that any seeming mistakes of my past are now transformed into my good."

"When I look at this situation in the rearview mirror of life, I will see how the CSO turned this situation into my good."

"I bless, love, and forgive everyone, and everyone blesses, loves, and forgives me. I bless, love, and forgive myself."

"There are no mistakes in the all-knowing power; therefore, there are no mistakes in my life."

"I now look into the rearview mirror of life and see that all situations had to happen in order for me to experience my higher and greater good now. All is well, and I gratefully go forward to prosper and be free."

It's important that you choose words that make you feel emotional and excited. Modify the statements above so that they have more meaning for you.

ACKNOWLEDGMENTS

This book could not have been possible without the support and love of so many of my family and friends. I'd like to thank my sister, Reverend Sharon Ramey, for encouraging me in all of my endeavors and for being a wonderful minister to answer my questions about new thought spiritual principles. A big thank you goes out to my other eight siblings, Sheila, Ann, Mor, Chris, Paul, Tom, Tim and Joe, for always being responsive to my prayer requests on the family text thread. I'm so grateful to my husband Don who has been called on repeatedly to read through my thoughts on paper and give me his honest impressions and feedback. Thank you to Randy Davila, Allison McDaniel and the entire staff at Hierophant Publishing for believing in me and the material in this book. I'm grateful to Laura Matthews for her tough questioning to clarify my use of the new thought spiritual principles to help others in achieving their dreams. A special thank you to the members of my Blessed Women Sangha whose faith and strength supported me in creating this book. And, to Rev. Dr. Kathianne Lewis and all of the ministers in Centers for Spiritual Living, Unity, and Universal Foundation for Better Living Churches around the world, I am so very grateful for the great work that you're doing. I see that your efforts are helping more people to understand their magnificent power to create a wonderful life for themselves and a world that works for everyone. Finally, I am most grateful to the thousands of readers, audience members, and workshop attendees who I've had the pleasure of meeting over the past few years as I've traveled the world. The stories about your experiences have encouraged me and directly influenced the creation of this book. Blessings and love to you all!

ABOUT THE AUTHOR

Since 1982, May McCarthy has co-founded and grown seven successful companies in a variety of industries to as large as 250 employees with over $100 million in annual revenues. She has also worked for Fortune 500 companies such as Johnson & Johnson and Boeing in sales and capital equipment purchasing, contracting, and barcode logistics design. As part of McCarthy's passion for entrepreneurship, she is the chair of the board for the Seattle University Innovation and Entrepreneurship Center, an active angel investor, and an advisor to dozens of start-up companies. She also serves on boards for business, philanthropic, arts, and nonprofit service organizations.

May McCarthy knows that her increasing success, fun, and growth are due to her partnership with the Divine. She shares her experience with others through her work as an author, professional speaker, and executive consultant who travels the world with the purpose of elevating prosperity and freedom for all. She meets daily with her CSO. May McCarthy lives in Texas with her husband Don Smith and their cat, Indy.

Learn more about May McCarthy here:

Facebook:
www.facebook.com/pages/May-Mccarthy/601413533280571

LinkedIn:
www.linkedin.com/pub/may-mccarthy/4/a55/b47/

Twitter:
www.twitter.com/maymcc

ALSO BY MAY McCARTHY:

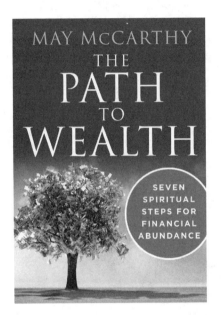

Available wherever books are sold.

books that inspire your body, mind, and spirit

Hierophant Publishing
8301 Broadway, Suite 219
San Antonio, TX 78209
888-800-4240

www.hierophantpublishing.com